THE WRITER'S
RHYMING DICTIONARY

D1605980

by

LANGFORD REED

Introduction by
JOHN HOLMES

Boston   THE WRITER, INC.   *Publishers*

PRINTED IN THE UNITED STATES OF AMERICA

RHYME IS A POWER

by JOHN HOLMES

A GOOD RHYMING DICTIONARY is a necessary part of any poet's working library. This rhyming dictionary is a good one, and what I like about it is that it is natural, small, and sensible. Without claiming to include all the words in the English language, it does contain a great many more than are in the ready rhyming vocabulary of most poets. The ready rhyming vocabulary is a highly specialized part of the poet's acquired equipment. He builds it up out of his preferences for the sound of words, throwing away the trite rhymes, individualizing his own choices, and always by adding more, hoping that his ready rhymes will come so swiftly when needed that they will not delay the rush of the poem itself. He should not repeat rhyme-sounds conspicuously in his poems, and so he must go on finding new ones. The function of a rhyming dictionary is to offer all there are, for the poet's need when it is desperate.

There is a right time, and a right way, to use a rhyming dictionary, which means that there is a way to think about a rhyming dictionary, an attitude toward the existence of such a book. It will not make a poet. It is only a word-list, after all. The poet's real rhyming vocabulary is in his head, and is of the color and movement of his own temperament, and even his physical make-up. When he is working on a poem, the poem stands first—the feel of the poem, the meaning, the new construction and existence he can make real if the materials obey him—and nothing else matters but the poem. To be stopped for a hunt for a rhyme can be disastrous, but disaster will not come for a while. Best of all, the rhyme should come without effort, without a book's help, and can often be foreseen, then put in place in the sentence, and the poem kept moving toward its climax. But it is possible, and even pleasurable, to suspend this rush, and fit the right rhyme in place. This is the time for the rhyming dictionary.

Suppose a rhyme is needed for the word *fern*. This rhyming dictionary is alphabetized by the sound of syllables—not by the spelling, but by the sound—and the sound wanted occurs alphabetically first as *earn*. One quickly and easily finds his way in this little book, riffling the pages past *earch, eard, earl,* to *earn,* which as a sound is also spelled *ern,* and *urn*. Place-names won't do, like *Berne* and *Lucerne,* and perhaps not particularized things like *intern, urn,* or *querne*. But who knows? They might suit, or they might suddenly enrich the metaphor the poem needs. Certainly there are verbs usable, like *learn, burn, turn*. Poets run through the alphabet in their heads, saying the sound with successive letters before it, but are not likely to get all there are. The rhyming dictionary has them all, and all before the eye. Something might work, and the poem can go on. The poem is first, rhyme subordinate.

But suppose nothing works, in the given list. It should be instantly recognized, known in a flash as the word that was wanted and almost known, or it is not much good to the poem. If no flash comes, then the poet must resist changing the poem for the sake of a second-best rhyme. The risk in using a rhyme-list is that one might use it because it's there, and shift the meaning of the poem so that it becomes something he never meant to write. This is disaster, or a crime against truth, but need not happen. If nothing works in the list, for the word *fern,* then the only thing to do is to re-write the lines so they do not require a rhyme. The mechanics of our language is flexible enough that no sentence-form is unvariable. The poet is master. Words and grammar work for him, not the other way round. Rhyme serves. It serves to decorate, to punctuate, to strengthen the poem's pattern, but only that. It is not the poem and should never dictate the meaning and direction of the poem.

After one has worked a while with a rhyming dictionary and come to know what can be found in it, as well as where to find it, he more or less realizes that some of the contents has become part of his working memory. There are words with too few rhymes to be of any use, because they have been used again and again, beyond surprise. *Ife* has only *fife, rife, knife, strife, life,* and *wife,* and the obvious combinations are ludicrous and boringly familiar. This list includes the word *life,* one that a poet would often be using or writing about. Like it, the word *death* has a poverty of rhymes, and the words *cold* and *old* are not much better off. Commonness of rhyme, the overworn use of the same old pairs, is to be avoided altogether. On the other hand, our language has too many rhymes for some words, too many for inclusion in this dictionary. If the preterites of certain words were to be printed here, the book would be for the shelves, not the table or pocket. The sound *ind,* (long), and *ined,* when listed as sounds, shows seventeen rhyme-words, not a very long list, with *bind, blind, kind, remind, grind,* and a few more in it. But there are also the preterites of verbs in *ign* and *ine,* as in *signed* and *dined,* and this longer list of rhyme-sounds created with word-endings must be made up. This dictionary lists large numbers of words ending in *ive* (short), like *narrative, give,* and *talkative;* and the same for the sounds *ist, est,* and *y,* which are endings. It also points out that there are about a thousand false rhymes in *less* and *ness,* that is, rhyme-words made by adding these sounds, not nouns and verbs like *stress, suppress, dress,* or *profess.* For the useful rhyme-sound *ose* (long) we are given *nose, oppose, transpose* and about forty more, and are told that we may, for more than sixty other good rhymes, see plurals of nouns and third person singulars of verbs in *o, ow,* and *oe.*

This suggests that many hundreds of rhymes cannot be included in a rhyming dictionary, and that they must come from the writer's own supply and making. Once we learn from this book what serviceable lists it contains, what principles of word-formation it teaches, and what sounds are in short supply or in profusion, we begin to feel our personal or ready rhyming vocabulary is larger, and actively growing. Each poet must eventually make his own rhyming dictionary, because his rhyming vocabulary is a distinctive part of his style, just as his imagery is, and nothing of the poet's is more consciously individualized, more ingeniously nourished, more jealously guarded, than his style. That is why a poet, using a rhyming dictionary, will take from it, not write by it. He will reject quantities of it, as not suiting his style, and will add what he does take to the body of his own vocabulary. His own rhyming dictionary, his perfect, unique list, is probably much smaller than the present book, and exists not even in editions of one copy each, but in his head. Some poets work deliberately at it, writing out long lists of rhymes in the back of notebooks, but this is another way of transferring them into the head.

The first part of this book is an alphabetical arrangement by rhyme-sounds of one-syllable rhymes, that is, one-syllable words that rhyme, or words in which the final, and accented, syllable is a rhyme. By choice, which probably means by temperament, by one's own pitch of nervous energy, the poet will use more one-syllable rhymes than any other, the kind that clearly, identically chime, and end the line or the poem on the beat. The second part of this book contains two-syllable rhymes, from *jabbered, scabbard, tabard,* through *coiner, joiner, purloiner,* to *lytham, rhythm, Witham.* By two-syllable rhymes is meant the likeness of both syllables. It is true that those just given are all there are in the language for these three sounds, and it seems true that they aren't very useful, though that might be personal. There are a great many small groups of sounds as two-syllable rhymes, but very few in a group. Perhaps this part of the book is more useful to writers of light verse. But when the need for a rhyme-word is serious, it is more difficult to remember or find as a two-syllable sound than as a one-syllable sound. The larger number of two-syllable rhymes do not have an accent on the last syllable, and these inevitably are lighter words in meaning and effect as well as sound, than the one-syllable rhymes. But all two-syllable rhymes are by no means comic, and it would be a monotonous style in poetry that never varied from the finality of the accented one-syllable rhyme. The English language, however, is characteristically one of falling rhythm, that is, we speak in iambics much of the time, and end a phrase or sentence on an accented syllable. The rhyming dictionary reveals the proportion of one- to two-syllable rhymes, or provides them for use.

By dividing this collection of rhyme-words into two parts, the one- and the two-syllable sounds, this dictionary does not take account in any way of the uses of rhyme, or the varying and more unusual kinds of rhyme. Masculine rhyme has one accented syllable, as *sun-done,* or *understand-land.* Feminine rhyme follows an accented syllable with an unaccented syllable, as *never-ever,* or *rural-plural.* These are the fundamental, usual kinds of rhyme. Both kinds are used as internal rhyme, one occurring at the middle as well as the end of a line. When rhymes close a line, they are called end-rhymes. The placement of rhyme at the beginnings of lines is a rare device, though Wilfred Owen uses it effectively, as a one-word line alternating with a much longer line, also rhymed. Alliteration is or was called initial rhyme. Sometimes, for emphasis, the same word is used as rhyme, rhyming with itself, and this is called identical rhyme. When words that were once pronounced alike have changed, the later age calls them historical rhymes, as when Pope rhymes *tea* with *away.* We no longer use what are called eye-rhymes, in which the spelling is alike and the sound actually different, as in *enough-cough.* But these are matters of the simpler kind, among which the poet chooses, as he may use them to invent a rhyme-scheme, perhaps mixing feminine and masculine.

English is not as rich in rhymes as Italian, or French, and our poets have experimented with variations on full masculine and feminine rhyme, to extend the ease and freedom of expression, and to enrich the music of the poem. One of these is light rhyme, as in *her-gather,* which pairs a stressed and an unstressed syllable because they have the same sound. Assonance is a rhyme using like vowels but unlike consonants, as in *flake-save.* Its opposite, consonance, is widely used, perhaps because the change of vowel is noticeable and still a pleasing musical effect, while the same consonants emphasize the subtle difference. *Tone-tune* is consonance, also called suspended rhyme, half rhyme, dissonance, and oblique rhyme. Its use multiplies by five or more the possibilities of rhyme for any end-word. Thus *tone* could be rhymed, if the intent of one's poem allowed, with *train, seen, fine, when, din,* and all the words that are exact rhymes with these sounds, an enormous gain in rhyming vocabulary. However, the effect of consonance as a rhyme is still light, unresolved, and this effect must be considered. Often it is best to use consonance at the ends of lines that alternate with exactly rhymed lines, a group being perhaps *tone-crush-fine-rush.* Consonance can also be feminine, like *ponder-sender, furnished-varnished,* and this makes an especially rich pair when alternated with masculine end-rhymes. With such combinations, and others more elaborately subtle, the poet may wish to experiment, as Emily Dickinson did, and Archibald MacLeish. The resulting effects will be an intensely personal quality of style, a trademark, and both to the poet and his reader a pleasure.

But rhyme should not be used when it is a hindrance, as it is to beginners who have not yet developed a rhyming vocabulary of their own. The lack of ready rhyme blocks them, and the poem they are capable of writing is lost. It is better to write honestly in spontaneous cadenced phrases without rhyme, than in forced and outworn rhyme. Later, when the poet feels more strongly the need for the discipline of form, he will try rhyme, but he will make every effort not to let it hamper him. To subordinate pattern, rhythm, metaphor, and rhyme to the poem itself, and make them all serve in concert the only purpose the poet may have, is to deserve the term poet. They have always rebelled against rhyme, though. The sixteenth and seventeenth centuries echo with outcry against it, and the objection is alive now. But it is an objection against restriction of any sort, not against rhyme as such. Rhyme mastered is not restrictive.

Richard Wilbur says, "Aside from the obvious value in the finished poem as a part of poetic form and as a heightener of language, rhyme seems to me an invaluable aid in composition. It creates difficulties which the utterance must surmount by increased resourcefulness. It also helps by liberally suggesting arbitrary connections of which the mind may take advantage if it likes. Rhyme, if austerely used, may be a stimulus to discovery and a stretcher of attention." This is the view of a poet whose craft is the admiration of many in his generation, and it states the best of the arguments for rhyme. When he speaks of rhyme creating difficulties, he implies excitement and delight in the response of his resourcefulness to the need. Rhyming, and making it work, is one of the satisfactions of writing poetry. That it stretches the reader's attention, something his ear must help with, is one of the extra advantages of rhyme. Peter Viereck, another contemporary, talks in metaphor about it, saying, "Rhyme and meter are the unchanging stage on which the changing actors stumble or dance. By keeping rhyme regular, I can provide a background which, by contrast, makes more effective the utmost variety, change, and imaginative flight. When rhyme and rhythm become too irregular, there is no contrast to spotlight the goings-on of the actors on the stage. This regularity demands the vowels of the full-vowelled rhymes to be the same." And John Frederick Nims says, of rhyme, "I like it as musical and formal. Pleasant in itself, unless used clumsily, it encloses and shapes; it emphasizes. More subtly, it connects in our mind the rhyming words and hence can fuse or juxtapose or contrast."

That the rhyming words in a poem can fuse, as Nims says, or juxtapose or contrast, by being remembered as a series of connected sounds that in itself says something, is a reference to the whole structure of a poem, in which the pattern has taken the shape of the thought, so that all the parts have their separate necessities. In part of a poem by William Dickey, the end-rhymes are *court, sty, counterpart, eye, sport, by.* It is the sestet of a sonnet and is a picture of a medieval court. *Court* is the first end-rhyme, and the next four are also nouns. The reality of each one adds to the particularity of the picture given, and with a sharpness like the vivid line of the painter. The end-rhyme of the last line is a subordinate part of the phrase, and the whole line, "And the perilous, delicate huntsmen riding by," is, like the huntsmen, also subordinate to the picture described. It might be pointed out here that there is another sort of contrast in rhymes, the difference in vowel-sound, necessary if the ear is to hear either set of rhymes. If the poet had rhymed *court-force-counterpart-horse-sport-source,* the likeness would be monotonous and confusing, even though he had one *-art* rhyme. A vowel-contrast is needed in exact rhyming, and whether he thought about it or not, the poet got it, in the long-*i* sound of *sty, eye, by,* set against the full, round *-or* sounds.

"Rhyme, though, remains a problem, especially to a writer like me," says E. L. Mayo, "who venerates the old patterns as channels worn through the deserts of human speech by the form-hungry imagination. For nothing is more depressing than a banal rhyme. And the Norn who provided the English language with its miraculous resources, withheld—just to balance matters, I suppose—one gift which most of the Romance languages take for granted: the gift of a multiplicity of rhyme words. Beginners in poetry are apt to adopt one of two mistaken courses: to employ rhyme-clichés until their verses jingle intolerably, or else to throw rhyme out of the window altogether and write prosy free verse (a poetic medium which requires above all a delicate and experienced "ear"). I am not sure which course is the more dangerous but I think likely the former, because at least the free-verse writer is brought up more sharply against his own deficiency. All this by way of saying that inner rhyme, slant rhyme, assonance, consonance, alliteration and the rest seem to be the ways by which the best modern poets escape from this dilemma. My own practice is to employ enough true rhyme to suggest regularity but no more. Used thus, rhyme is helpful in establishing stanza form, as a device for emphasis and in general for the control of the overall sound structure." This is a good time to remind new poets that free verse is not necessarily unrhymed. It is stubbornly rooted in popular conviction that free verse is chopped-up prose, without plan, without rhyme, without any of the structure of meter and sound that is vital to poetry. The word verse means turn, or cut lengths, and is used of free verse to say that it is freely cut, that is, in lines of varying length. What determines the length is phrase, either by its meaning and its unity of grammar, or by breath needed to say it; and sometimes for emphasis by placement, the single word, the series of three-word lines. The freedom to end lines where the sense and the voice suggest it makes heavy demands on dramatic instinct, on the ear that hears the poem as if spoken, and even on the eye that sees the poem as design on the page. Nothing says free verse may not be rhymed, but neither does it say how to rhyme it. Free verse certainly may be freely rhymed, and again it is an instinct for climax, a structural feeling that knows where re-enforcement is needed, that tells the poet where to put the rhyme. Of course there is no fixed pattern. Each free verse poem is its own pattern, never so shaped before, and never to be so shaped again. Each is an original, and there is no mould. This is why Mayo says free verse runs the danger of being prosy, in inexperienced hands. It is not the easiest, but rather the hardest of poetry to write well.

"Rhyme as an automatic structural device, automatically attended to, is attractive to me, but I like it best irregular, live, and heard," says Randall Jarrell. This is the comment of a man who makes rhyme serve him, obviously, but service is not enough. When he says he likes it best "irregular, live, and heard," he gives it the greatest structural importance in the architecture of the poem, presumably his own. He acknowledges more than the well-finished rhyme-pattern. He admits he makes rhyme give thrust, surprise, and force to his poem. The poets quoted here, on rhyme, agree with extraordinary likeness on most aspects of the matter. It is not that they consulted one another, but that they have learned from poetry itself, as they have labored to make their several styles. They were answering, however, the same set of questions or suggestions, proposed by John Ciardi to the fifteen poets he wished to include in his *Mid-Century American Poets,* as to their attitudes toward the technical problems of writing. In spite of considerable agreement among them, the learning poet can get more of what he wants from reading their poetry, with these statements in mind, than from the statements alone. They are as different from one another as they are in personal appearance. How does rhyme become part of their poetry? Their books provide the example. Ciardi himself says "Rhyme, internal as well as line-end, is not an appliquéd ornamentation, but part of the total voice-punctuation of the poem. It is one way, along with 'sense,' line-length, punctuation, and rhythm, that the poet controls the reader's voice, leading him to speak the piece as the poet heard it. In many cases, this effect is best achieved by irregular rather than regular rhyme."

Whether these and other poets agree as to irregularly placed rhyme or not, or rhyme as an aid in composition, or as structural punctuation, it is clear that such purposes lie back of the choice of rhyming words. It is with such stylistic principles in mind, such integrities of art, that the learning poet uses a rhyming dictionary. It is the chief virtue of this one that it can be used with a quickly found expertness, like a good tool that fits the hand, and tells the workman by its shape what it is for. The rhymes wanted are where they are expected to be.

The title of this introduction comes from Karl Shapiro's long poem, "Essay On Rime," lines 791 and following. (He prefers the very old spelling, as it was in Middle English; the dictionaries now call it a variant of our word *rhyme,* and I have used the familiar spelling.) Shapiro writes:

> In the mathematical sense, rime is a power,
> Prose raised to the numerical exponent
> Of three or six or even *n,* depending
> Upon the propensity of the literature
> At a particular time and on the bent
> Of the particular poet. It is therefore
> A heightening and a measure of intensity.

Some reference has been made, as in the matter of eye-rhyme and historical rhyme, to "the propensity of the literature at a particular time." Much more has been said about "the bent of the particular poet." Each of the contemporary poets quoted on their attitudes to the use of rhyme has his particular bent. I have indicated what the bent of a particular poet and user of this dictionary should be by saying he must choose and adapt from these word-lists, according to his poem's needs and to his own developing style. But about rhyme as a power, I agree with Shapiro, who says further that it is the nuclear and vital element, in the physical sense; the protoplasm of the tongue, in the biological sense; and in the theological sense, the ghost, and prose the flesh of language.

PART I
ONE-SYLLABLE RHYMES

ONE-SYLLABLE RHYMES

A, AH

Ah	baa	bah	blah
ha	la	ma	pa
Shah	ta	faux-pas	holla
hurrah	mama	papa	algebra
cinema	fistula		

(And many other false rhymes ending in "a," such as "America," "Corsica," etc.)

AB

abb	blab	cab	crab
dab	drab	gab	grab
jab	Mab	nab	scab
slab	stab	tab	confab
Punjab			

ABE

Abe	babe	astrolabe	outgrabe
			(Lewis Carroll)

AC, ACK

bac	back	black	cack
clack	claque	crack	hack
jack	Jack	knack	lac
lack	"mack"	Mac	pack
plaque	quack	rack	sac
sack	shack	slack	smack
snack	stack	tack	thwack
track	whack	wrack	yak
aback	alack	almanac	Appotomac
attack	bric-a-brac	cardiac	demoniac
drawback	gimcrack	haversack	horseback
hyperchondriac	knapsack	maniac	ransack
Sarawak	stickleback	zodiac	

3

ACE, ASE

ace	base	bass	brace
case	chase	dace	face
grace	Grace	lace	mace
pace	place	plaice	race
space	Thrace	trace	abase
bullace	debase	deface	disgrace
displace	efface	embrace	grimace
horse-race	interlace	interspace	market-place
misplace	outface	outpace	populace
replace	retrace	staircase	transplace
uncase	unlace		

ACH, ATCH

batch	catch	hatch	latch
match	patch	ratch	scratch
slatch	snatch	thatch	attach
dispatch	detach	unattach	unlatch

(For rhymes to "watch," see OTCH.*)*

ACHE *(see* AKE*)*   ACK *(see* AC*)*

ACT

act	fact	pact	tact
tract	abstract	attract	cataphract
cataract	co-act	compact	contact
contract	counteract	detract	distract
enact	epact	exact	extract
impact	infract	overact	protract
react	refract	retract	retroact
subtract	transact		

(Extend ACK *for "blacked" and other preterites.)*

AD

ad	bad	brad	cad
chad	clad	dad	fad
gad	glad	had	lad
mad	pad	plaid	sad
shad	Bagdad	bedad	footpad
ironclad	olympiad	monad	nomad

(For rhymes to "wad," "squad" and "quad," see OD.*)*

ADE, AID

aid	bade	blade	braid
cade	fade	glade	grade
jade	lade	laid	made
maid	neighed	paid	plaid
raid	shade	skaid	Slade
sleighed.	spade	stade	staid
they'd	trade	wade	weighed
abrade	accolade	afraid	ambuscade
arcade	balustrade	barricade	Belgrade
blockade	brigade	brocade	cannonade
cascade	cavalcade	citigrade	cockade
colonnade	comrade	crusade	decade
degrade	dissuade	enfilade	escalade
esplanade	evade	fusillade	gasconade
grenade	housemaid	invade	lemonade
marmalade	masquerade	mermaid	nightshade
okayed	orangeade	overlade	overlaid
palisade	parade	pasquinade	persuade
pervade	plantigrade	renegade	retrograde
serenade	stockade	underlaid	unlade
unlaid	unmade	unpaid	upbraid
waylaid			

(Also "flayed," "grayed," and many other preterites of verbs ending in AY *and* EY, *which see.*)

ADGE

badge	cadge	fadge	Madge

ADZE

adze (*see plurals of words in* AD)

AFE

chafe	Rafe	safe	waif
unsafe	vouchsafe		

AFF

gaff	Taff	autograph	behalf
carafe	cenotaph	cinematograph	distaff
epitaph	giraffe	Llandaff	paragraph
phonograph	photograph	riff-raff	telegraph
seraph			

5

AFT

aft	chaffed	craft	daft
draft	draught	graft	haft
Kraft	laughed	quaffed	raft
shaft	staffed	"straffed"	waft
abaft	autographed	cinematographed	handicraft
paragraphed	photographed	telegraphed	understaffed

AG

bag	brag	crag	dag
drag	fag	flag	gag
hag	jag	knag	lag
nag	quag	rag	sag
scrag	shag	slag	snag
stag	swag	tag	wag
zigzag			

AGE

age	cage	Drage	gage
gauge	page	rage	sage
stage	swage	wage	assuage
disengage	greengage	presage	

(And nearly 100 false rhymes in words ending in AGE in which the final syllable is not accentuated, such as "sausage," "advantage.")

AGUE

Hague	plague	Prague	vague

AID (see ADE)

AIL, ALE

ail	ale	bail	bale
brail	dale	fail	flail
frail	gale	Grail	hail
hale	jail	kail	kale
mail	male	nail	pail
pale	quail	rail	sail
sale	scale	shale	snail
stale	swale	tail	tale
they'll	trail	vale	veil
wale	whale	wail	Yale
assail	avail	bewail	blackmail

6

bobtail	countervail	curtail	detail
entail	exhale	farthingale	female
impale	inhale	nightingale	prevail
regale	retail	travail	unveil
wagtail	wassail	wholesale	

AIM, AME

aim	blame	came	claim
dame	fame	flame	frame
game	lame	maim	name
same	shame	tame	acclaim
became	declaim	defame	disclaim
exclaim	inflame	overcame	nickname
proclaim	reclaim	surname	

AIN, ANE

ain (*Scotch*)	bane	blain	brain
Cain	cane	chain	crane
Dane	deign	drain	fane
fain	feign	gain	grain
Jane	lain	lane	main
Maine	mane	pain	pane
plain	plane	rain	reign
rein	sane	Seine	skein
slain	Spain	sprain	stain
strain	swain	thane	train
twain	vain	vane	vein
wain	wane	abstain	airplane
again	amain	appertain	arraign
attain	biplane	campaign	chamberlain
champagne	chicane	chilblain	cocaine
complain	constrain	contain	detain
disdain	distrain	domain	Elaine
enchain	engrain	entertain	entrain
explain	fountain	germane	henbane
humane	hurricane	inane	legerdemain
Louvain	maintain	membrane	monoplane
mountain	murrain	obtain	ordain
pearmain	pertain	plantain	porcelain
profane	ptomaine	refrain	regain
remain	restrain	retain	sustain
terrain			

AINT

aint	faint	feint	mayn't
paint	plaint	quaint	saint
taint	acquaint	attaint	complaint
constraint	distraint	restraint	

AIR, ARE

air	Ayr	bare	bear
blare	care	chair	Claire
Clare	dare	e'er	ere
fare	flair	flare	fair
gare	hair	hare	heir
glare	lair	mare	mayor
Herr	pair	pare	pear
ne'er	rare	scare	share
prayer	spare	square	stair
snare	swear	tare	tear
stare	there	ware	wear
their	yare	affair	armchair
where	beware	co-heir	compare
aware	commissionaire	concessionaire	corsair
compere	declare	Delaware	despair
debonair	elsewhere	ensnare	fanfare
eclair	forswear	howe'er	unfair
forbear	millionaire	mohair	nightmare
Mayfair	repair	unaware	prepare
welfare	whate'er	whene'er	unfair

AIRD

Baird	braird	Caird	laird

(And preterites of verbs in previous list; thus bared.)

AIRN

bairn	cairn	Nairn

AISE, AYS, AIZE, AZE

baize	blaze	braise	craze
chaise	daze	gaze	glaze
graze	haze	laze	maize
maze	naze	phase	phrase
praise	raise	raze	traits
yeas	ablaze	amaze	appraise

(And add "s" to words ending in AY and EY, which see.)

8

AIT, ATE, EIGHT

ait	ate	bait	bate
crate	date	eight	fate
fête	freight	gait	gate
grate	great	hate	Kate
late	mate	pate	plait
plate	prate	rate	sate
skate	slate	spate	state
straight	strait	trait	weight
abate	abdicate	abominate	abrogate
accelerate	accentuate	accommodate	accumulate
acerbate	acidulate	adulterate	advocate (*verb*)
aggravate	aggregate	agitate	alienate
animate	annotate	antedate	anticipate
arbitrate	arrogate	articulate	aspirate
cachinate	calculate	candidate	capacitate
capitulate	captivate	casemate	castigate
celebrate	checkmate	cicurate	coagulate
collate	commemorate	commiserate	communicate
compassionate	compensate	complicate	confiscate
congratulate	congregate	conjugate	consecrate
consolidate	contaminate	contemplate	co-operate
correlate	corroborate	create	cremate
crenelate	cultivate	debate	debilitate
dedicate	delegate	deliberate	demonstrate
denominate	depopulate	depreciate	derogate
detonate	dilate	discriminate	dislocate
dissipate	duplicate	educate	ejaculate
elaborate	elate	elevate	elucidate
equivocate	eradicate	estate	estimate
expectorate	expostulate	exterminate	extricate
fabricate	facilitate	felicitate	formulate
fornicate	frustrate	generate	germinate
gyrate	hesitate	hibernate	illuminate
imprecate	incubate	indicate	ingrate
initiate	innate	innovate	inoculate
instigate	intimate	intimidate	intricate
inundate	invalidate	investigate	irate
irrigate	irritate	lacerate	liquidate
litigate	lubricate	macerate	machinate
magistrate	matriculate	mediate	meditate
migrate	militate	mitigate	moderate

9

modulate	mutilate	narrate	nauseate
navigate	necessitate	nominate	oblate
orate	ornate	oscillate	oscitate
osculate	participate	penetrate	percolate
perforate	personate	placate	postulate
potentate	precipitate	predicate	predestinate
predominate	premeditate	prevaricate	procrastinate
profligate	propagate	prostrate	reciprocate
recriminate	regulate	reiterate	remonstrate
reprobate	reverberate	ruminate	rusticate
satiate	saturate	sedate	separate
spiflicate	stipulate	subjugate	subordinate
suffocate	syndicate	tabulate	terminate
tête-à-tête	titivate	tolerate	translate
triturate	ultimate	underrate	vacate
variegate	ventilate	venerate	vindicate

(*And many false rhymes in words ending in* ATE *short.*
Thus "adequate," "effeminate," etc.)

AITH

faith	wraith

AKE

ache	bake	brake	break
cake	crake	drake	fake
flake	hake	Jake	lake
make	quake	rake	sake
shake	slake	snake	spake
stake	steak	strake	take
wake	awake	bespake	betake
corn crake	forsake	keepsake	mandrake
mistake	namesake	opaque	overtake
partake	snowflake	sweepstake	undertake

AL

chal (*Romany*)	mal	pal	Sal
shall	cabal	canal	Natal

(*And more than* 100 *false rhymes in words ending in* AL
in which the final syllable is not accentuated, such as
"animal," "historical," etc.)

AL (*long*)

Transvaal (*and compare* ARL)

ALC

talc   catafalque

ALD

bald   scald   Archibald   piebald

(And about twenty preterites of verbs ending in ALL, AUL *and* AWL, *which see.)*

ALE *(see* AIL)   ALF *(see* AFF *long)*

ALK, AUK, AWK

auk	balk	baulk	calk
chalk	gawk	hawk	stalk
talk	walk	Dundalk	tomahawk

(Compare ORK.)

ALL, AUL, AWL

all	awl	ball	bawl
brawl	call	caul	crawl
drawl	fall	gall	Gaul
hall	haul	maul	pall
Paul	pawl	Saul	scrawl
shawl	small	sprawl	squall
stall	tall	thrall	trawl
wall	yawl	appal	Bengal
baseball	enthral	football	install
Nepal	overhaul	rainfall	snowfall
waterfall	Whitehall	windfall	

ALM, ARM

alm	arm	balm	barm
calm	charm	farm	harm
palm	psalm	qualm	smarm
alarm	becalm	embalm	disarm
gendarme	madame	salaam	

ALP

alp   scalp

ALSE

false   valse   waltz

ALT, AULT

fault	halt	malt	salt
vault	assault	cobalt	default
exalt			

ALVE (*silent* L)

calve	halve

(*Compare* ARVE.)

ALVE (L *sounded*)

salve	valve	bivalve

AM

am	Cam	Cham	clam
cram	dam	damn	drachm
dram	flam	gram	ham
jam	jamb	lam	lamb
mam	pam	pram	ram
Sam	sham	slam	swam
yam	anagram	Amsterdam	Assam
Rotterdam	Siam		

And many false rhymes, including

bantam	beldam	cryptogram	diagram
diaphragm	epigram	madam	monogram
oriflamme	Surinam	telegram	wigwam

AME (*see* AIM)

AMP

amp	camp	champ	clamp
cramp	damp	gamp	lamp
ramp	scamp	stamp	tramp
vamp	decamp	encamp	

(*For rhymes to* "swamp," *see* OMP.)

AN

an	Anne	ban	bran
can	clan	Dan	fan
flan	khan	Jan	man
pan	Pan	plan	ran

scan	span	tan	**than**
van	Afghanistan	began	Deccan
divan	Hindostan	Japan	sedan
trepan	Turkestan		

*(And about 100 false rhymes in words in which the final
syllable is not accentuated. Thus "African," "Puritan,"
"courtesan.")*

ANCE, ANSE

chance	dance	France	glance
lance	manse	prance	stance
trance	advance	askance	enhance
entrance	mischance	romance	seance

*(And about 30 false rhymes in words, ending in ANCE in
which the final syllable is not accentuated, thus "am-
bulance," "vigilance," etc.)*

ANCH

blanch	Blanche	branch	ganch
ranch	stanch	carte-blanche	

AND

and	band	bland	brand
gland	grand	hand	land
rand	Rand	sand	stand
Strand	strand	command	contraband
countermand	demand	expand	reprimand
Sunderland	understand	unhand	withstand
wonderland			

*(And preterites of verbs ending in AN, which see. For
rhymes to "wand," see OND.)*

ANE (*see* AIN)

ANG

bang	bhang	clang	fang
gang	hang	Lang	pang
rang	sang	slang	sprang
stang	tang	twang	harangue
meringue	orang-outang	Penang	

13

ANGE

change	grange	mange	range
strange	arrange	estrange	exchange
interchange			

ANK

bank	blank	brank	clank
crank	dank	drank	flank
franc	frank	Frank	hank
lank	plank	prank	rank
sank	shank	spank	stank
swank	tank	thank	twank
yank	Yank	embank	disrank
mountebank			

ANT

ant	bant	brant	can't
chant	grant	pant	plant
rant	scant	shan't	slant
aslant	descant	displant	enchant
implant	Levant	recant	supplant
transplant			

(*And about 50 false rhymes by wrongly accentuating the final syllables of such words as "arrogant," etc. For rhymes to "want," see* ONT.)

ANX

francs	Lancs	Manx

(*And pluralize words ending in* ANK.)

AP

cap	chap	clap	dap
flap	frap	gap	hap
Jap	knap	lap	map
nap	pap	rap	sap
scrap	slap	snap	strap
tap	trap	wrap	yap
entrap	enwrap	kidnap	madcap
mishap			

14

APE

ape	cape	Cape	chape
crape	dape	drape	gape
grape	jape	nape	rape
scrape	shape	tape	trape
escape			

APES

traipse   jackanapes

    (*And add "s" to above.*)

APH (*see* AFF)

APSE

apse	lapse	elapse	**collapse**
perhaps	relapse		

    (*And add "s" to words under* AP.)

APT

apt   rapt   adapt

    (*And preterites of twenty-two verbs ending in* **AP, which**
      see.)

AQUE (*see* ACK)

AR

are	bar	car	char
czar	far	jar	mar
par	scar	spar	star
tar	afar	bazaar	Calabar
Candahar	catarrh	caviar	cigar
debar	disbar	Dunbar	felspar
Forfar	guitar	hussar	Navarre
Zanzibar			

    (*And a number of false rhymes, by wrongly accentuating
      the final syllables of such words as "popular."*)

ARB

barb   garb   rhubarb

ARCE, ARSE

carse   farce   sparse

(For rhymes to "parse," pluralize some words in AR.)

ARCH

arch	larch	march	March
parch	starch		

ARD

bard	card	guard	hard
lard	nard	pard	shard
yard	bombard	body-guard	discard
petard	regard	reynard	disregard
interlard			

(And extend AR *for "barred" and other preterites. For rhymes to "Ward," see* OARD.)

ARE (*as in "rare," see* AIR)

ARF (*broad*)

dwarf   wharf

ARGE

barge	charge	large	marge
sparge	targe	discharge	surcharge

ARK

arc	ark	bark	barque
cark	clerk	dark	hark
lark	mark	Mark	marque
nark	park	Sark	shark
"Snark	spark	stark	embark
hierarch	Irak	landmark	matriarch
patriarch	Perak	remark	

ARL, AAL

Basle	carl	Carl	gnarl
marl	snarl	taal	Transvaal

ARM (*see* ALM)

ARN

barn	darn	"garn!"	Larne
Marne	stern (*nautical*)	tarn	yarn

ARP

carp	harp	scarp	sharp
Zarp	counterscarp		

ARSE

parse (*And add "s" to words in*   ras (*Abyssinian chief*)
   AR)

ARSH

harsh	marsh	moustache

ART

art	bart	cart	chart
dart	hart	heart	mart
part	smart	start	tart
apart	counterpart	depart	dispart
impart	rampart	sweetheart	upstart

ART (*as in "quart," see* ORT)

ARVE

ave	carve	starve	suave
Zouave			

(*Compare* ALVE.)

AS, AZZ

as	has	jazz	"razz"
La Paz			

ASE (*see* ACE)

ASH

ash	bash	brash	cache
cash	clash	crash	dash
fash (*Scotch*)	flash	gash	gnash
hash	lache	lash	mash
Nash	pash	plash	rash
sash	slash	smash	splash
tache	thrash	trash	abash
sabretache	Saltash		

17

ASH (*as in "wash"*)

quash	squash	wash	musquash

And slang words, as follows:

Boche	bosh	cosh	gosh
josh	posh	slosh	splosh
tosh			

ASK

ask	bask	Basque	cask
flask	Jask	mask	task

ASM

chasm	plasm	spasm	cataplasm
protoplasm	enthusiasm	miasm	phantasm
sarcasm			

ASP

asp	clasp	gasp	grasp
hasp	rasp		

ASS

ass	bass	brass	crass
gas	grass	has	lass
mass	pass	alas	amass
coup-de-grace	cuirass	Madras	morass
repass	surpass	unclass	

AST

blast	cast	caste	fast
gassed	hast	last	massed
mast	past	vast	aghast
avast	bombast	contrast	cuirassed
enthusiast	forecast	iconoclast	metaphrast
outcast			

(*And preterites of verbs in* ASS, *as in "passed."*)

18

ASTE

baste	chaste	haste	paste
taste	waist	waste	distaste
unchaste			

(*And preterites of many verbs in* ACE *and* ASE, *as in* "based" *and* "disgraced.")

AT

at	bat	brat	cat
chat	drat	fat	flat
gnat	"gat"	hat	Jat
mat	pat	Pat	plait
plat	rat	sat	slat
spat	sprat	tat	that
vat	acrobat	Ballarat	combat (*verb*)
Herat	loquat	Montserrat	polecat
tit-for-tat			

ATE (*see* AIT)   ATCH (*see* ACH)

ATH

bath	Bath	Gath	hath
hearth	lath	math	path
"rath" (*Lewis Carroll*)	scath	aftermath	bypath
	Penarth		

ATHE

bathe	athe	scathe	swathe

AUB, ORB

daub	orb	Taube	absorb

AUD

bawd	broad	Claude	fraud
gaud	laud	Maud	abroad
applaud	defraud		

(*And many preterites of verbs in* AW, *as* "clawed." *Compare* OARD *and* ORDE.)

AUGH (*see* AFF)

AUGHT and OUGHT

aught	bought	brought	caught
fought	fraught	naught	nought
ought	sought	taught	taut
wrought	besought	bethought	distraught
forethought	methought	overwrought	

(*Compare* ORT.)

AUK, AULK and AWK (*see* ALK)   AUN (*see* AWN)

AUNCH

haunch	launch	paunch	staunch

AUNT (*broad*)

chaunt	daunt	gaunt	haunt
jaunt	taunt	vaunt	avaunt

AUSE, AUZE

awes	cause	clause	gauze
pause	tawse	applause	because
turquoise			

(*And add "s" to certain words in* AW.)

AV

have	Slav

AVE

brave	cave	crave	Dave
drave	gave	grave	knave
lave	nave	pave	rave
save	shave	slave	stave
they've	trave	waive	wave
architrave	behave	conclave	deprave
engrave	enslave	forgave	margrave
octave	outbrave		

AW

awe	caw	chaw	claw
craw	daw	draw	flaw
gnaw	haw	jaw	law
maw	paw	pshaw	raw
saw	Shaw	squaw	straw
taw	thaw	yaw	foresaw

cat's-paw	Choctaw	guffaw	jackdaw
macaw	overawe	usquebaugh	withdraw
Warsaw			

AWK (see ALK) AWL (see ALL)

AWN

awn	bawn	brawn	dawn
drawn	faun	fawn	lawn
pawn	prawn	sawn	spawn
yawn	withdrawn		

(Compare ORN.)

AX

claques	flax	lax	Max
pax	plaques	sax. (for saxo-	tax
wax	borax	climax phone)	parallax
relax	thorax		

(And see AC and ACK and add "s.")

AZ

as	has	jazz

(And see under AS.)

AZE (see AISE)

AY, EY

bay	bey	bray	Bray
clay	day	dey	dray
drey	eh	fay	fey
flay	fray	gay	gray
grey	hay	jay	lay
leh	may	May	nay
née	neigh	pay	play
pray	prey	ray	say
shay	slay	sleigh	Spey
spray	stay	stray	sway
Tay	they	trait	tray
trey	way	weigh	whey
yea	affray	array	assay
astray	belay	betray	Bombay
cabaret	café-au-lait	cabriolet	convey
decay	defray	déjeuner	delay
disarray	dismay	disobey	display

21

doomsday	embay	essay	gainsay
gangway	hearsay	Herne Bay	heyday
hooray	inlay	inveigh	Malay
mid-day	mislay	Moray	obey
okay	negligée	portray	purvey
relay	repay	replay	survey
Torbay	Tokay	waylay	

(And more than thirty false rhymes, such as "highway," "Monday," "popinjay," etc.)

E, EA, EE

be	bee	Cree	Dee
dree	fee	flea	flee
free	gee	glee	he
key	knee	lea	lee
Lee	Leigh	me	"oui"
pea	plea	quay	sea
see	she	ski	spree
Spree	tea	tee	thee
three	tree	we	wee
ye	absentee	agree	Ashantee
bohea	cap-a-pie	chimpanzee	coterie
coo-ee	debauchee	debris	decree
degree	devotee	disagree	Dundee
fricassee	fusee	grandee	grantee
jamboree	jeu-d'esprit	legatee	lessee
licensee	mortgagee	nominee	"on dit"
oversea	Parsee	patentee	pedigree
pharisee	pugaree	recipe	referee
refugee	repartee	Sadducee	settee
squeegee	Torquay	trustee	vendee
vis-à-vis	Zuyder Zee		

(And many false rhymes in words ending in "y"; thus "history," peremptory," etc.)

EACE, EASE

cease	crease	creese	fleece
geese	grease	Greece	lease
Nice	niece	peace	piece
caprice	decease	decrease	frontispiece
increase	mantelpiece	masterpiece	obese
police	release	surcease	verdigris

EACH

beach	beech	bleach	breach
breech	each	leech	peach
preach	reach	screech	speech
teach	beseech	impeach	outreach

EAD (*short, see* ED)

EAD (*long*), EDE, EED

bead	bleed	breed	cede
creed	deed	feed	freed
glebe	greed	heed	keyed
knead	lead	mead	Mede
meed	need	plead	read
reed	screed	seed	speed
steed	swede	Swede	teed
treed	tweed	Tweed	weed
accede	agreed	antecede	centipede
concede	decreed	disagreed	exceed
filigreed	guaranteed	impede	indeed
intercede	knock-kneed	linseed	misdeed
mislead	precede	proceed	recede
refereed	reparteed	secede	stampede
succeed	supersede	velocipede	

EAF (*short*), EF

chef	clef	deaf

EAF (*long, see* EEF)

EAGUE, IGUE

Greig	league	teague	colleague
fatigue	intrigue		

EAK, EEK, IQUE

beak	bleak	cheek	chic
clique	creak	creek	eke
freak	Greek	leak	leek
meek	peak	peek	pique
reek	seek	sheik	shriek
Sikh	sleek	sneak	speak
squeak	streak	teak	tweak
weak	week	wreak	antique
bespeak	bezique	critique	unique

23

EAL, EEL

creel	deal	Deal	eel
feel	heal	heel	he'll
keel	Kiel	leal	meal
Neal	peal	peel	real
reel	seal	she'll	skeel
squeal	steal	steel	streel
sweal	teal	veal	weal
we'll	wheel	zeal	anneal
appeal	automobile	chenille	cochineal
commonweal	conceal	congeal	deshabille
genteel	ideal	imbecile	profile
repeal	reveal	unreal	

EALD, IELD

field	shield	weald	wield
yield			

(And preterites of verbs in previous list.)

EALM

elm	helm	realm	whelm
overwhelm			

EALTH

health	stealth	wealth	commonwealth

EAM, EEM

beam	bream	Cheam	cream
deem	dream	gleam	ream
scheme	scream	seam	seem
steam	stream	team	teem
theme	abeam	beseem	blaspheme
disesteem	esteem	redeem	supreme

EAMT, EMPT

dreamt	kempt	tempt	attempt
contempt	exempt	unkempt	

EAN, EEN

bean	been	clean	dean
e'en	glean	green	jean

keen	lean	lien	mean
mesne	mien	quean	queen
scene	screen	seen	sheen
spleen	teen	wean	ween
yean	aniline	between	bombazine
brigantine	canteen	careen	chlorine
Christine	Clementine	colleen	convene
contravene	crinoline	demean	Doreen
eighteen	Eileen	evergreen	fifteen
fourteen	gabardine	Geraldine	gelatine
go-between	guillotine	intervene	iodine
Jacqueline	kerosene	machine	MacLean
magazine	margarine	misdemean	nectarine
nicotine	nineteen	obscene	overseen
quarantine	quinine	routine	saccharine
sardine	seccotine	serene	seventeen
shagreen	shebeen	sixteen	sordine
spalpeen	submarine	tambourine	tangerine
terrene	tontine	tureen	ultramarine
umpteen	unclean	unforeseen	unseen
vaseline	velveteen	zebrine	

EAND, IEND

fiend   (*And preterites of some verbs in previous list.*)

EANT (*see* ENT)

EAP, EEP

cheap	chepe	clepe	creep
deep	heap	jeep	keep
leap	neap	peep	reap
sheep	sleep	steep	sweep
threap	weep	asleep	overleap

EAR, EER, EIR, ERE, IER

beer	bier	blear	cere
cheer	clear	dear	deer
drear	ear	fear	fleer
gear	hear	here	jeer
Lear	leer	mere	near
peer	pier	queer	rear
sear	seer	shear	sheer
"skeer"	smear	sneer	spear

25

sphere	steer	tear	tier
vere	veer	weir	year
adhere	appear	atmosphere	auctioneer
austere	bandoleer	brigadier	bombardier
buccaneer	carabineer	career	cashier
Cashmere	cavalier	chandelier	chanticleer
charioteer	chevalier	chiffonier	cohere
commandeer	compeer	disappear	domineer
endear	engineer	fusilier	gazetteer
gondolier	grenadier	halberdier	hemisphere
inhere	insincere	interfere	mountaineer
muleteer	musketeer	mutineer	overhear
overseer	pamphleteer	persevere	pioneer
privateer	profiteer	rehear	reindeer
revere	scrutineer	severe	sincere
sonneteer	Tangier	uprear	veneer
volunteer	Windermere		

(*And "Algiers" for plurals.*)

EARCH, ERCH, IRCH, URCH

birch	church	Kertch	lurch
perch	search	smirch	besmirch
research			

EARD (*short*), ERD, IRD, URD

bird	curd	gird	heard
herd	Kurd	sherd	surd
third	word	absurd	administered
massacred	ministered	registered	

(*And preterites of many verbs in ER, IR, and UR, which see.*)

EARD (*long*), EIRD

beard	weird

(*And more than forty preterites of verbs in EAR, EER and ERE, which see.*)

EARL, IRL, URL

churl	curl	earl	furl
girl	hurl	pearl	purl
skirl	twirl	whirl	uncurl
unfurl			

26

EARLED, IRLED, ORLD

world

(And preterites of verbs in previous list.)

EARN, ERN, URN

Berne	burn	churn	earn
erne	fern	hern	kerne
learn	querne	spurn	stern
tern	turn	urn	yearn
adjourn	astern	concern	discern
intern	Lucerne	overturn	return
sojourn	unconcern	unlearn	

EARSE (*see* ERCE)   EART (*see* ART)

EARTH, ERTH, IRTH

berth	birth	dearth	earth
firth	girth	mirth	Perth
worth			

(For rhymes for "hearth," see ATH.)

EASE (*as in "lease," see* EACE)

EASE (*soft*), EEZE, ISE

breeze	Caius	cheese	ease
freeze	frieze	Guise	grease (*verb*)
mise	please	seize	skis
sneeze	squeeze	tease	these
appease	Burmese	cerise	chemise
Chinese	Japanese	Louise	Maltese
Portuguese	Pyrennees	Siamese	trapeze
Tyrolese	valise	Viennese	

(And see EA and EE for many plurals, thus "fleas," "fees.")

EAST, IEST

beast	east	feast	least
priest	yeast	artiste	

(And preterites of verbs in EACE and EASE, soft, which see. For rhymes to "breast," see EST.)

27

EAT, EET, EIT, ITE

beat	beet	bleat	cheat
cleat	Crete	eat	feat
feet	fleet	greet	heat
meat	meet	mete	neat
peat	Pete	pleat	seat
sheet	skeet	sleet	street
suite	sweet	teat	treat
wheat	complete	conceit	deceit
defeat	discreet	discrete	effete
elite	entreat	escheat	incomplete
indiscreet	obsolete	petite	repeat
replete	retreat	secrete	

(For rhymes to "great," see AIT)

EATH (*short*)

Beth	breath	death	saith
Seth			

EATH (*long*)

heath	Leith	Meath	neath
Neath	sheath	teeth	wreath
beneath	bequeath	Blackheath	Dalkeith
underneath	unsheathe		

EATHE

breathe	seethe	sheathe	teethe
wreathe	bequeath		

EAVE, EIVE, EVE, LEVE

beeve	cleave	eave	eve
Eve	greave	grieve	heave
leave	lieve	peeve	reeve
screeve	sheave	sleeve	Steve
thieve	vive	weave	we've
achieve	aggrieve	believe	bereave
conceive	deceive	disbelieve	interleave
perceive	preconceive	receive	relieve
reprieve	retrieve	undeceive	unweave

28

EB, EBB

bleb	ebb	Feb.	neb
reb	web	Webb	

ECK

beck	check	cheque	Czech
deck	fleck	"heck"	neck
peck	reck	sec	speck
trek	wreck	bedeck	henpeck
Quebec	zebec		

ECT

sect	abject	adject	affect
architect	bisect	circumspect	collect
conflect	connect	correct	defect
deflect	deject	detect	dialect
direct	disaffect	disconnect	disinfect
elect	erect	expect	incorrect
infect	insect	inspect	intellect
interject	intersect	introspect	neglect
object	pandect	perfect	prefect
project	prospect	protect	recollect
reflect	reject	respect	retrospect
select	subject	suspect	traject
vivisect			

(And preterites of verbs in ECK, *which see.)*

ED, EAD *(short)*

bed	bled	bread	bred
dead	dread	fed	fled
Fred	head	lead	led
Ned	pled	read	red
said	shed	shred	sled
sped	spread	stead	Ted
thread	tread	wed	abed
ahead	behead	bedstead	blockhead
bulkhead	gingerbread	instead	loggerhead
misled	trucklebed	unread	unsaid

(Also preterites and past participles ending in ED *when the final syllable is accentuated, as in "visited.")*

EDE *(see* EAD, *long)*

29

EDGE

edge	dredge	fledge	hedge
kedge	ledge	pledge	Reg (*for Regi-*
sedge	sledge	veg. (*for vege-*	wedge *nald*)
allege	privilege	sacrilege	*tables*)

EE (*see* E)   **EECE** (*see* EACE)

EECH (*see* EACH)   **EED** (*see* EAD)

EEF, IEF

beef	brief	chief	crief
fief	feof	grief	leaf
lief	reef	sheaf	thief
bas-relief	belief	disbelief	enfeoff
handkerchief	misbelief	neckerchief	unbelief

EEK (*see* EAK)   **EEL** (*see* EAL)

EEM (*see* EAM)   **EER** (*see* EAR)

EESE (*see* EASE)   **EET** (*see* EAT)

EFT

cleft	deft	eft	heft
left	theft	weft	bereft

EG

beg	clegg	dreg	egg
keg	leg	Meg	peg
seg	skeg	"yegg"	nutmeg
philabeg			

EGM (*see* EM)   **EIGN, EIN** (*see* AIN)

EL, ELLE

bell	belle	cell	dell
dwell	ell	fell	hell
knell	Nell	quell	sell
shell	smell	spell	swell
tell	well	yell	asphodel

bagatelle	befell	calomel	caramel
citadel	cockerel	compel	Cornell
debel	dispel	doggerel	Estelle
excel	expel	farewell	foretell
gazelle	hotel	impel	infidel
lapel	mackerel	muscatel	parallel
pell-mell	philomel	rebel	repel
rondel	sentinel	undersell	villanelle

ELD

eld	geld	held	weld
beheld			

(And preterites of some verbs in previous list.)

ELF

delf	delph	elf	Guelph
pelf	self	shelf	himself
herself	myself	thyself	yourself

ELK

elk	whelk	yelk

ELM (*see* EALM)

ELP

help	kelp	skelp	whelp
yelp			

ELT

belt	Celt	dealt	dwelt
felt	Kelt	knelt	melt
pelt	smelt	spelt	svelte
veldt	welt		

ELVE

delve	helve	shelve	twelve

EM

gem	hem	Jem	phlegm
Shem	stem	them	apothegm

31

| condemn | contemn | diadem | requiem |
| theorem | stratagem | | |

("*Thames*" *for plurals.*)

EME (*see* EAM)   EMPT (*see* EAMT)

EMP

| hemp | kemp | | |

EN

Ben	den	fen	glen
hen	ken	men	pen
sen	ten	then	wen
when	wren	yen	

ENCE, ENSE

dense	fence	hence	pence
sense	tense	thence	whence
commence	commonsense	condense	defense
dispense	expense	immense	incense
intense	offense	prepense	pretense

(*And over* 100 *false rhymes by accentuating the final syllables of such words as* "*impertinence*," "*reference*.")

ENCH

bench	blench	clench	drench
French	quench	stench	tench
trench	wench	wrench	intrench

END

bend	blend	end	fend
friend	kenned	lend	mend
penned	rend	send	spend
tend	trend	vend	wend
amend	append	apprehend	ascend
attend	befriend	commend	compend
comprehend	condescend	contend	defend
depend	descend	discommend	distend
dividend	expend	extend	forfend
impend	intend	misapprehend	misspend
offend	Ostend	portend	pretend
propend	recommend	reprehend	reverend
South End	superintend	suspend	transcend

32

ENGTH

length	strength

ENS

cleanse	ens	lens

(Add "s" to words in EN.*)*

ENSE *(see* ENCE)

ENT

bent	Brent	cent	fent
gent	Kent	lent	Lent
meant	pent	rent	scent
sent	spent	tent	Trent
vent	went	absent (*verb*)	accent (*verb*)
acquent	anent	ascent	assent
augment	cement	circumvent	comment
consent	content	descent	dissent
event	extent	ferment	foment
frequent	indent	intent	invent
lament	misspent	present (*verb*)	prevent
repent	represent	resent	unbent

(And more than 200 *false rhymes, by accentuating the final syllables of such words as "penitent," "sapient," etc.)*

EPP

nep	pep	"prep"	repp
skep	step	yep	Dieppe
demirep			

(Pluralize to rhyme with "Schweppes" and "steppes.")

EPT

crept	kept	leapt	pepped
Sept.	slept	stepped	swept
wept	accept	adept	concept
except	inept	intercept	overslept
precept	yclept		

ER, IR, UR

blur	burr	cur	err
fir	fur	her	knur
myrrh	per	purr	sir
slur	spur	stir	whir

astir	aver	bestir	concur
defer	demur	deter	douceur
infer	inter	occur	prefer
recur	refer	transfer	

(And about 70 false rhymes, by accentuating the final syllables of such words as "arbiter," "forager," etc.)

ERB, URB

curb	blurb	herb	kerb
Serb	verb	ascerb	disturb
perturb	superb		

ERCE, ERSE, URSE

curse	Erse	hearse	nurse
purse	terse	verse	worse
adverse	ammerce	asperse	averse
coerce	commerce	converse	disperse
diverse	imburse	immerse	intersperse
inverse	perverse	precurse	rehearse
reimburse	reverse	sesterce	subverse
transverse	traverse	universe	

ERD (*see* EARD)   ERE (*see* EAR)

ERF, URF

scurf	serf	surf	turf

ERGE, IRGE, URGE, OURGE

dirge	merge	purge	scourge
serge	splurge	surge	urge
verge	converge	deterge	diverge
emerge			

ERK, IRK, URK

burke	Chirk	dirk	irk
jerk	kirk	lurk	merk
murk	perk	quirk	shirk
smirk	Turk	work	yerk
Albuquerque			

ERM, IRM

firm	germ	Herm	perm
sperm	squirm	term	therm
worm	affirm	confirm	infirm

ERN (*see* EARN)   ERSE (*see* ERCE)

ERT, IRT, URT

Burt	blurt	cert	curt
dirt	flirt	Gert	girt
hurt	pert	"quirt"	shirt
skirt	spurt	squirt	vert
wert	advert	alert	animadvert
assert	avert	concert	controvert
convert	desert	dessert	disconcert
divert	exert	expert	filbert
Gilbert	incontrovert	inexpert	assert
invert	malapert	obvert	overt
pervert	revert	subvert	unhurt

ERTH (*see* EARTH)

ERVE, URVE

curve	nerve	serve	swerve
turves (*pl. of turf*)	verve	conserve	deserve
observe	preserve	reserve	subserve
unnerve			

ES, ESCE, ESS

Bess	bless	cess	chess
cress	dress	fesse	guess
less	mess	ness	press
stress	Tess	tress	yes
abscess	acquiesce	actress	address
aggress	ambassadress	assess	caress
coalesce	compress	confess	depress
digress	dispossess	distress	duress
editress	excess	express	effervesce
finesse	giantess	impress	Inverness
lioness	manageress	marchioness	mayoress
nevertheless	noblesse	obsess	overdress
patroness	politesse	possess	prepossess
princess	prioress	profess	progress

prophetess	proprietress	recess	redress
repossess	repress	sheerness	sorceress
success	suppress	transgress	undress

(And about 1,000 false rhymes in LESS and NESS. Thus, "uselessness.")

ESH

flesh	fresh	mesh	nesh
thresh	afresh	enmesh	refresh

ESK, ESQUE

desk	Esk	arabesque	burlesque
grotesque	moresque	picturesque	romanesque
statuesque			

EST

best	blest	breast	Brest
chest	crest	guest	jest
lest	nest	pest	quest
rest	test	vest	west
wrest	zest	abreast	arrest
attest	behest	bequest	Budapest
congest	contest	detest	digest
infest	inquest	interest	invest
manifest	molest	obtest	protest
reinvest	request	suggest	unblest

(And preterites of many verbs in ESS, which see. Also a number of false rhymes in which the accent is not on final syllable, such as "conquest," etc.)

ET, ETTE

ate	bet	Cette	debt
fret	get	jet	ket
let	met	net	pet
set	stet	sweat	threat
vet	wet	yet	abet
alphabet	amulet	bassinet	beset
cadet	corvette	castanet	chansonette
cigarette	coquette	curvet	duet
epaulette	epithet	etiquette	falconette
flannelette	floweret	forget	gazette
grisette	lazarette	leveret	lunette
maisonette	marionette	marmoset	martinet

36

mignonette	minaret	minuet	Nannette
novelette	offset	omelette	overset
parapet	piquet	pierette	pirouette
quadruplet	quartette	quintet	regret
rosette	sarcenet	serviette	sextette
Somerset	suffragette	Thibet	upset

ETCH

etch	fetch	ketch	fletch
retch	sketch	stretch	vetch
wretch	outstretch		

ETE (*see* EAT)   EVE (*see* EAVE)   EUD (*see* OOD)

EW, IEU, UE (*with diphthong*)

cue	dew	due	ewe
few	gnu	hew	hue
lieu	mew	new	pew
queue	slew	spew	stew
strew	sue	Sue	view
yew	you	adieu	anew
askew	avenue	Baku	barbecue
bedew	bellevue	beshrew	curfew
curlew	emu	endue	ensue
mildew	parvenu	purlieu	pursue
renew	residue	retinue	review
revenue	subdue	venue	

EW, UE (*no diphthong*) *and* OO

blew	blue	boo	brew
chew	clew	clue	coup
crew	Crewe	do	drew
flew	flue	glue	goût (*taste*)
grew	loo	Lou	moo
rue	screw	shoe	shrew
slew	strew	sou	thew
threw	through	to	too
true	two	who	woo
you	zoo	accrue	ado
bamboo	billet-doux	canoe	cockatoo
construe	cuckoo	debut	entre-nous
kangaroo	misconstrue	Peru	ragout
rendezvous	shampoo	surtout	taboo

EX

cheques	Exe	flex	Rex
sex	"specs"	treks	vex
annex	circumflex	codex	complex
convex	index	perplex	reflex

(Also the present tense of verbs and the plurals of nouns in ECK, as in "decks" and "wrecks")

EZ

fez	Fez	sez	Les. *(for Leslie)*

I *(see Y)*

IAR

(As in "liar," see two-syllable rhymes.)

IB

bib	crib	dib	drib
fib	glib	jib	nib
quib	rib	squib	

IBE

bribe	gibe	gybe	kibe
scribe	tribe	ascribe	circumscribe
describe	diatribe	imbibe	inscribe
prescribe	proscribe	subscribe	superscribe
transcribe			

IC, ICK

brick	chick	click	crick
Dick	flick	hick	kick
lick	Mick	nick	pick
prick	quick	rick	sic
sick	slick	snick	spick
stick	thick	tic	tick
trick	Vic	wick	Wick

And false rhymes as follows:

arsenic	bishopric	candlestick	catholic
caustic	choleric	fiddlestick	heraldic
heretic	impolitic	lunatic	Pickwick
plethoric	politic	rhetoric	

38

ICE, ISE (*short*)

bice	dice	ice	lice
mice	nice	price	rice
slice	spice	splice	thrice
trice	twice	vice	advice
concise	device	entice	precise
sacrifice	suffice		

ICH (*see* ITCH) ICK (*see* IC)

ICT

Pict	strict	addict	afflict
benedict	conflict	constrict	contradict
convict	depict	edict	evict
interdict	predict	relict	restrict

(*And preterites of verbs in* ICK, *which see.*)

ID

bid	chid	Cid	did
grid	hid	kid	lid
mid	quid	rid	skid
slid	squid	thrid	yid
amid	eyelid	forbid	Madrid
outbid	pyramid	underbid	

IE (*see* Y)

IDE, IED

bide	bride	chide	Clyde
glide	gride	guide	hide
Hyde	pride	ride	Ryde
side	slide	snide	stride
tide	wide	abide	aside
astride	backside	backslide	beside
betide	broadside	Christmastide	collide
coincide	confide	decide	deride
divide	elide	eventide	fratricide
homicide	infanticide	insecticide	inside
matricide	misguide	noontide	parricide
preside	provide	regicide	reside
subdivide	suicide	tyrannicide	

(*Also "cried," "died," "signified," and about* 70 *other preterites of verbs in* Y, IE *and* YE, *which see.*)

IDES

besides   ides

(And add "s" to words in previous list.)

IDGE

| bridge | midge | ridge | abridge |
| cartridge | partridge | privilege | sacrilege |

IDST

bidst	chidst	didst	hidst
midst	ridst	slidst	amidst
forbidst			

IEF (*see* EEF)

IEGE

liege   siege   besiege

IEND (*see* EAND)   IER (*see* EAR)

IELD (*see* EALD)

IERCE

| fierce | Pearce | pierce | tierce |

IEVE (*see* EAVE)

IF, IFF, YPH

biff	cliff	glyph	if
niff	quif	"Riff"	skiff
sniff	stiff	tiff	whiff

IFE

| fife | Fife | knife | life |
| naif | rife | strife | wife |

IFT

clift	drift	gift	lift
rift	shift	sift	swift
thrift	adrift	snowdrift	spendthrift
uplift			

(And preterites of verbs in IF.*)*

40

IG

big	brig	dig	fig
gig	grig	jig	pig
prig	rig	snig	sprig
swig	twig	Whig ·	wig
periwig	whirligig		

IGH (*see* Y)   IGHT (*see* ITE)   IGN (*see* INE)

IKE

bike	dyke	hike	Ike
like	Mike	pike	shrike
spike	strike	tyke	alike
dislike	Klondyke	mislike	turnpike
unlike	Vandyke		

IL, ILL

bill	Bill	brill	chill
dill	drill	fill	frill
gill	grill	grille	hill
ill	Jill	kill	mill
nil	pill	quill	rill
skill	spill	squill	still
swill	thrill	till	trill
twill	'twill (*it will*)	will	Will
Brazil	codicil	daffodil	distill
downhill	Evansville	freewill	fulfil
instil	quadrille	Seville	until
uphill	watermill		

ILCH

filch	milch	pilch

ILD (*short*)

build	gild	guild	rebuild

(*And preterites of verbs in* IL, *as in* "billed.")

ILD (*long*)

child	mild	wild

(*And preterites of verbs in* ILE, *thus* "filed," "exiled.")

41

aisle	bile	chyle	file
guile	I'll	isle	mile
Nile	pile	rile	smile
stile	style	tile	vile
while	wile	Anglophile	Argyle
Carlyle	compile	crocodile	defile
diastyle	exile	Francophile	domicile (*verb*)
gentile	infantile	juvenile	mercantile
peristyle	puerile	reconcile	revile
servile	tensile		

ILK

bilk	ilk	milk	silk

ILN

biln	kiln	Milne

ILT

built	gilt	guilt	hilt
jilt	kilt	lilt	quilt
silt	spilt	milt	stilt
tilt	wilt	rebuilt	unbuilt

ILTH

filth	spilth	tilth

IM

brim	dim	glim	grim
him	hymn	Jim	limb
limn	Lympne	prim	rim
skim	slim	swim	Tim
trim	Trim	vim	whim
bedim	cherubim	interim	pilgrim
pseudonym	Sanhedrim	seraphim	synonym

IME

chime	chyme	climb	clime
crime	dime	grime	lime
Lyme	mime	prime	rhyme
rime	slime	thyme	time
overtime	pantomime	sublime	
IMES (*pluralize above*)		sometimes	

42

IMP

blimp	"chimp"	crimp	gimp
imp	jimp	limp	pimp
"simp"	shrimp	skimp	

IMPSE

glimpse   *(And pluralize words in above list.)*

IN, INN, INE *(short)*

bin	chin	din	djinn
fin	Finn	Glynne	gin
grin	in	inn	kin
lyn	Lynn	pin	quin
shin	sin	skin	spin
thin	tin	twin	whin
win	akin	begin	Berlin
cannikin	chagrin	Corinne	culverin
discipline	feminine	finickin	harlequin
herein	heroine	jacobin	javelin
jessamine	kilderkin	libertine	mandarin
mandolin	mannequin	minikin	origin
paladin	palanquin	peregrine	ravelin
therein	unpin	violin	wherein
within			

INCE

mince	prince	quince	rinse
since	wince	convince	evince

INCH

cinch	clinch	finch	flinch
inch	lynch	pinch	winch

INCT, INKED

tinct	distinct	extinct	indistinct
instinct	precinct	succinct	

(And preterites of verbs in INK, as in "blinked.")

IND *(short) and* INNED

Scinde	wind	abscind	rescind
tamarind			

*(And preterites of verbs in IN and INE, as in "pinned" and
"disciplined.")*

43

IND (*long*) *and* INED

bind	blind	find	grind
hind	kind	mind	rind
wind	behind	gavelkind	mankind
purblind	remind	unkind	unwind
womankind			

(*And preterites of verbs in* IGN *and* INE, *as in* "signed" *and* "dined.")

INE

brine	chine	dine	eyne
fine	kine	Klein	line
mine	nine	pine	Rhine
shine	shrine	sign	sine
spine	Stein	swine	syne
thine	tine	Tyne	trine
twine	vine	whine	wine
align	alkaline	anodyne	aquiline
Argentine	asinine	assign	brigantine
Byzantine	calcine	canine	carbine
carmine	celandine	Clementine	columbine
combine	concubine	condign	consign
coastline	countermine	crystalline	decline
define	design	disincline	divine
eglantine	elephantine	enshrine	entwine
feline	incardine	incline	indign
interline	intertwine	iodine	leonine
malign	moonshine	opine	outline
outshine	palatine	porcupine	recline
refine	reline	repine	saline
saturnine	serpentine	sunshine	superfine
turpentine	underline	undermine	untwine
valentine	vesperine	woodbine	

ING

bring	cling	ding	fling
king	ling	Ming	ring
sing	sling	spring	sting
string	swing	thing	Thring
wing	wring	unsling	

(*And more than* 1,000 *false rhymes in present participles, as in* "happening," "issuing," *etc.*)

INGE

binge	cringe	fringe	hinge
singe	springe	tinge	twinge
astringe	befringe	impinge	infringe
syringe	unhinge		

INK

blink	brink	chink	clink
drink	gink	ink	kink
link	mink	pink	prink
rink	shrink	sink	skink
slink	stink	swink	think
tink	twink	wink	zinc
bethink	hoodwink	interlink	methink

INT (*short*)

dint	flint	Flint	glint
hint	lint	mint	print
quint	splint	sprint	squint
stint	tint	aquatint	asquint
imprint	peppermint	reprint	

(*No rhyme for "pint."*)

INTH

plinth	absinthe	Corinth	hyacinth
labyrinth			

INX, INKS

jinx	lynx	minx	sphinx
larynx			

(*And add "s" to nouns and verbs in* **INK.**)

IP

chip	clip	dip	drip
flip	gyp	grip	hip
kip	lip	nip	pip
quip	rip	scrip	ship
sip	skip	slip	snip
strip	tip	trip	whip
zip	equip	outstrip	tranship

45

apprenticeship	battleship	censorship
championship	citizenship	chaplainship
deaconship	dictatorship	fellowship
guardianship	horsemanship	ladyship
partnership	penmanship	scholarship
sizarship	stewardship	workmanship
	and etc.	

IPT

script manuscript

(*And preterites of verbs in* IP, *as in "snipped."*)

IPE

gripe	pipe	ripe	snipe
stripe	swipe	tripe	type
wipe	bagpipe	hornpipe	linotype
monotype	prototype	stereotype	unripe
windpipe			

IPSE, IPS

apocalypse eclipse ellipse

(*And add "s" to nouns and verbs in* IP, *as in "snips."*)

IQUE (*see* EAK)   IR   (*see* ER)

IRCH (see EARCH)   IRD (*see* EARD)

IRE, YRE

byre	choir	dire	fire
gyre	hire	ire	lyre
mire	pyre	quire	shire
sire	spire	tire	tyre
Tyre	wire	acquire	admire
attire	bonfire	conspire	desire
empire	entire	esquire	expire
grandsire	inspire	perspire	quagmire
require	respire	retire	sapphire
satire	suspire	transpire	

(*Compare* IAR *in list of two-syllable rhymes.*)

46

IRGE (*see* ERGE)   IRK (*see* ERK)

IRL (*see* EARL)   IRM (*see* ERM)

IRN (*see* EARN)

IRP, URP

chirp	twerp	extirp	usurp

(*Past tense to rhyme with "excerpt."*)

IRST, ERST, URST

burst	curst	durst	erst
first	Hurst	thirst	verst
worst	athirst		

(*And preterites of verbs in* ERCE, ERSE *and* URSE, *as in* "coerced," "versed" *and* "cursed.")

IRT (*see* ERT)   IRTH (*see* EARTH)

IS, ISS, ICE (*short*)

bis	bliss	Diss	hiss
kiss	miss	Swiss	this
wys	abyss	amiss	dismiss
remiss			

And false rhymes, as follows:

analysis	antithesis	apotheosis	armistice
artifice	benefice	chrysalis	cicatrice
cockatrice	cowardice	dentifrice	edifice
elephantiasis	emphasis	genesis	hypostasis
hypothesis	jaundice	liquorice	metamorphosis
metastasis	metropolis	necropolis	orifice
paralysis	parenthesis	precipice	prejudice
prolapsis	synthesis		

IS (*long*), IZ

biz	fizz	his	is
Liz	phiz	quiz	'tis
viz	whiz	Cadiz	

ISE, IZE

guise	prise	prize	rise
size	wise	acclimatize	advertise
anglicize	apologize	apostatize	apostrophize
apprise	arise	assize	astrologize
astronomize	authorize	baptize	barbarize
bastardize	Belsize	brutalize	canonize
carbonize	catholicize	cauterize	centralize
characterize	chastise	christianize	cicatrize
circularize	circumcise	citizenize	civilize
cognise	colloquialize	colonize	comprise
compromise	congenialize	contrariwise	criticise
crystallize	democratize	demoralize	deodorize
demise	dentize	despise	devitalize
devise	dialize	dichotomize	disguise
disorganize	dogmatize	economize	egotize
emblemize	emphasize	epigrammatize	epilogize
epitomize	equalize	etherealize	etymologize
eulogize	euphonize	evangelize	excise
exercise	exorcise	extemporize	externalize
familiarize	fanaticize	fertilize	feudalize
formalize	fossilize	franchise	fraternize
geometrize	gluttonize	gorgonize	gormandize
harmonize	heathenize	hellenize	humanize
immortalize	imperialize	improvise	individualize
internationalize	italicize	jeopardize	judaize
latinize	legalize	liberalize	likewise
localize	macadamize	magnetize	materialize
mechanize	mediatize	memorize	mercerise
merchandise	mesmerize	metalize	methodize
militarize	mineralize	minimize	misprize
mobilize	modernize	monopolize	moralize
nationalize	neutralize	nomadize	occidentalize
organize	orientalize	ostracize	otherwise
pauperize	philosophize	phlebotomize	plagiarize
pluralize	poetize	polarize	popularize
premise	protestantize	proverbialize	pulverize
puritanize	realize	recognize	regularize
reprise	revise	revolutionize	rhapsodize
romanize	ruralize	sanctuarize	satirize
scandalize	secularize	sensitize	sensualize
signalize	solescize	solemnize	soliloquize

spiritualize	standardize	summarize	atomize
televise	finalise	specialize	sunrise
surmise	syllogize	symbolize	sympathize
synchronize	synonymize	systematize	tantalize
temporize	terrorize	theorize	tranquilize
tyrannize	unwise	utilize	ventriloquize
victimize	visualize	vocalize	volatize
vulcanize	vulgarize	weatherwise	

(Also plurals of nouns in IGH *and third person singular of verbs in* Y. *Thus "thighs" and "tries." See under* Y.)

ISH

dish	fish	Nish	pish
squish	swish	wish	

And false rhymes, such as:

anguish	cleverish	devilish	feverish
gibberish	heathenish	impoverish	lickerish
liverish	willowish	womanish	yellowish

ISK

bisk	bisque	brisk	disk
frisk	risk	whisk	asterisk
basilisk	obelisk	odalisque	tamarisk

ISM

chrism	prism	schism	agnosticism
Americanism	anachronism	anarchism	aneurism
anglicism	aphorism	archaism	atheism
baptism	barbarism	bolshevism	calvinism
capitalism	Carrollism	cataclysm	catechism
catholicism	chauvinism	colloquialism	communism
conservatism	criticism	Darwinism	deism
despotism	dogmatism	egotism	empiricism
evangelism	exorcism	Fascism	fanaticism
feudalism	gallicism	heathenism	hedonism
heroism	hibernism	Hitlerism	hypnotism
Ibsenism	idealism	imperialism	Judaism
laconism	latinism	liberalism	libertinism
magnetism	malthusianism	mannerism	materialism
mechanism	mesmerism	methodism	modernism
nationalism	nepotism	occidentalism	occultism
optimism	organism	orientalism	ostracism
paganism	pantheism	paroxysm	patriotism

pauperism	pelmanism	pessimism	plagiarism
presbyterianism	protestantism	provincialism	puritanism
pyrrhonism	radicalism	rationalism	realism
rheumatism	ritualism	sabbatism	scepticism
Shavianism	socialism	solescism	stoicism
truism	vandalism	ventriloquism	vocalism
vulgarism	witticism	Zionism	

ISP

crisp   **lisp**   wisp

ISS (see IS, short)

IST, ISSED, YST

cist	cyst	fist	gist
grist	hist	list	mist
tryst	twist	whist	wist
wrist	academist	agriculturist	alchemist
amethyst	amorist	analogist	analyst
anarchist	anatomist	apologist	assist
atheist	baptist	beneficed	bicyclist
bigamist	bolshevist	botanist	calvinist
capitalist	casualist	casuist	catechist
chiropodist	chronologist	co-exist	colonist
colourist	columnist	communist	consist
dialist	desist	diarist	diplomatist
dismissed	dogmatist	dramatist	dualist
duellist	economist	egotist	emblematist
etymologist	eucharist	evangelist	exist
exorcist	externalist	fabulist	Fascist
fatalist	geologist	geometrist	hebraist
hedonist	hellenist	herbalist	humanist
humorist	hypnotist	idealist	idolist
imperialist	internationalist	insist	instrumentalist
intertwist	journalist	lapidist	latinist
loyalist	materialist	malthusianist	medallist
memoralist	mesmerist	metallist	metallurgist
meteorologist	methodist	militarist	mineralogist
moralist	motorist	mythologist	nationalist
naturalist	novelist	obstructionist	occidentalist
oculist	opinionist	ontologist	optimist
organist	orientalist	pathologist	pessimist
philanthropist	philatelist	philologist	phlebotomist

psychiatrist	physiognomist	physiologist	plagiarist
pluralist	pianist	pietist	polygamist
protectionist	psychologist	psychometrist	pugilist
pyrologist	pyrotechnist	rationalist	realist
receptionist	religionist	revivalist	revolutionist
rhapsodist	ritualist	royalist	satirist
secularist	schematist	scientist	sensualist
separatist	sexualist	socialist	soloist
spiritualist	suffragist	syncopist	tautologist
telegraphist	telephonist	terrorist	theologist
tobacconist	unionist	ventriloquist	violinist
visualist	vocalist	votarist	Zionist

(And preterites of verbs in ISS, *as in* "kissed.")

IT, ITE (*short*)

bit	chit	cit	fit
flit	grit	hit	it
kit	knit	lit	mitt
nit	pit	quit	sit
skit	slit	smit	spit
split	sprit	tit	twit
whit	wit	writ	acquit
admit	opposite	benefit	bowsprit
commit	definite	emit	exquisite
favourite	hypocrite	indefinite	infinite
intermit	intromit	Jesuit	manumit
omit	opposite	outwit	perquisite
permit	pewit	preterite	recommit
refit	remit	requisite	submit
titbit	transmit	unfit	

ITCH

bitch	ditch	fitch	flitch
hitch	itch	lych	niche
pitch	rich	snitch	stitch
switch	which	witch	bewitch
distich	enrich	hemstitch	

ITE (*long*), IGHT

bite	bight	blight	bright
cite	dight	fight	flight
fright	height	kite	knight

light	might	mite	night
pight	plight	quite	right
rite	sight	site	sleight
slight	smite	spite	sprite
tight	trite	white	wight
wright	write	accite	acolyte
aconite	affright	alight	anchorite
appetite	bedight	bedlamite	benight
biparite	candlelight	Carmelite	chrysolite
composite	cosmopolite	contrite	delight
despite	disunite	downright	dynamite
eremite	excite	expedite	foresight
hermaphrodite	impolite	ignite	incite
indict	insight	invite	Jacobite
midnight	midshipmite	moonlight	neophyte
outright	overnight	oversight	parasite
polite	proselyte	recite	requite
recondite	reunite	satellite	stalactite
stalagmite	starlight	sunlight	Sybarite
theodolite	troglodyte	twilight	underwrite
vulcanite	watertight	weathertight	zeolite
zincite			

ITE (*short*) *as in* "*definite*" (*see* IT)

ITH, YTH

fifth	frith	kith	myth
pith	sith	smith	with
withe	forthwith	herewith	monolith
Penrith	therewith	wherewith	zenith

ITHE

blithe	hithe	Hythe	lithe
scythe	tithe	writhe	

ITS, ITZ

Blitz	Fritz	Ritz

(*And plurals of words in* IT.)

IVE (*short*)

give	live	sieve	ablative
abdicative	abductive	accumulative	accusative
acquisitive	administrative	affirmative	alliterative

52

alternative	appelative	applicative	appreciative
argumentative	authoritative	causative	cogitative
commemorative	communicative	comparative	consecutive
conservative	contemplative	contributive	co-operative
copulative	correlative	corroborative	curative
curvative	declarative	decorative	definitive
degenerative	deliberative	demonstrative	depreciative
derivative	derogative	desiccative	determinative
diminutive	discriminative	distributive	emanative
eradicative	executive	explicative	figurative
fugitive	generative	genitive	illuminative
illustrative	imaginative	imitative	imperative
inchoative	indicative	infinitive	inquisitive
insinuative	instinctive	interrogative	intuitive
justificative	lambative	laxative	lenitive
lucrative	meditative	narrative	negative
operative	opinionative	palliative	perspective
persuasive	prejudicative	positive	performative
preparative	prerogative	preservative	primitive
privative	procreative	productive	progressive
prospective	provocative	punitive	purgative
putative	recitative	recreative	recriminative
refrigerative	regenerative	relative	remonstrative
remunerative	reparative	representative	restorative
retributive	reverberative	significative	speculative
substantive	superlative	talkative	tentative

IVE

Clive	dive	drive	five
gyve	hive	I've	live
naïve	rive	shive	shrive
strive	thrive	wive	alive
arrive	beehive	connive	contrive
deprive	derive	revive	survive

IX, ICS, ICKS

fix	mix	nix	pyx
six	strix	Styx	admix
affix	cicatrix	crucifix	executrix
intermix	matrix	onyx	prefix
prolix	sardonyx	transfix	unfix

(*And plurals of nouns in* ICK, *as in* "kicks.")

O, OW, EAU, OE

beau	blow	bow	co. (*company*)
crow	do (*music*)	doe	dough
Flo	floe	flow	foe
fro	glow	go	grow
ho	hoe	Joe	know
lo	low	mow	no
oh	owe	po	pro
roe	row	sew	shew
show	sloe	snow	stow
strow	though	throe	throw
toe	trow	woe	adagio
ago	allegro	although	apropos
banjo	below	bestow	braggadocio
bravo	bureau	buffalo	calico
cameo	chapeau	chateau	cocoa
comme il faut	de trop	depot	domino
duo	duodecimo	embryo	falsetto
forego	foreshow	furbelow	generalissimo
haricot	heigh-ho	hello	Idaho
imbroglio	incognito	indigo	intaglio
memento	mistletoe	mulatto	nuncio
oleo	Ontario	oratorio	outgrow
overgrow	overflow	overthrow	pierrot
Pimlico	pistachio	plateau	portico
rondeau	seraglio	Soho	stiletto
tobacco	torpedo	trousseau	undergo
vertigo	volcano		

OACH

broach	brooch	coach	loach
poach	roach	approach	cockroach
encroach	reproach		

OAD, ODE, OWED

bode	code	goad	load
lode	mode	node	ode
road	rode	strode	toad
commode	corrode	episode	erode
explode	forebode	incommode	

(*And preterites of verbs in* OE, OW *and* OWE; *thus "toed,"*
"towed" and "owed.")

54

OAF

loaf	oaf

OAK, OKE

bloke	broke	choke	cloak
coke	croak	folk	joke
moke	oak	poke	smoke
soak	spoke	stoke	stroke
toque	woke	yoke	yolk
artichoke	awoke	bespoke	convoke
equivoke	gentlefolk	invoke	masterstroke
provoke	revoke	unyoke	

OAL, OLE, OL, OLL, OUL, OWL

bole	bowl	coal	dole
droll	foal	goal	hole
jole	knoll	mole	pole
poll	role	roll	scroll
shoal	sole	soul	stole
stroll	thole	toll	troll
vole	whole	aureole	cajole
camisole	caracole	champagnol	condole
console	control	Creole	enrol
girandole	girasole	parole	patrol
petrol	pistole	rantipole	

OAM, OME

chrome	comb	dome	foam
Frome	gnome	holme	home
loam	"mome" (*Car-*	Nome	roam
Rome	tome *roll*)	aerodrome	catacomb
currycomb	hippodrome	palindrome	

OAN, ONE, OWN

bone	blown	cone	crone
drone	flown	groan	grown
hone	Joan	known	loan
lone	moan	own	prone
roan	Rhone	scone	shown
Sloane	sown	stone	strown
tone	throne	thrown	zone

55

alone	atone	bemoan	chaperone
Cologne	cornerstone	depone	dethrone
dictaphone	disown	enthrone	gramaphone
grindstone	intone	knucklebone	microphone
moonstone	ozone	postpone	telephone
undertone	unknown	unsewn	

OAR, ORE

boar	bore	core	corps
door	floor	fore	four
gore	hoar	lore	more
nore	Nore	o'er	pore
pour	roar	score	shore
snore	soar	sore	store
swore	tore	whore	wore
yore	war	adore	afore
ashore	battledore	before	Cawnpore
claymore	commodore	deplore	encore
evermore	explore	forbore	foreshore
forswore	furthermore	galore	heretofore
ignore	implore	matador	restore
sophomore	troubadour	semaphore	spoor

(*Compare* OR *and* OOR.)

OARD, ORED, ORD, ORDE

board	chord	cord	ford
hoard	horde	lord	sward
sword	ward	accord	harpsichord
record	reward		

(*Compare* AUD.) (*And preterites of verbs in previous
list.*)

OARSE (*see* ORCE)

OAST, OST (*long*)

boast	coast	ghost	grossed
host	most	post	roast
toast	almost	hindermost	innermost
lowermost	nethermost	outermost	undermost
uppermost			

OAT, OTE

bloat	boat	bote	coat
cote	Croat	dote	float
gloat	goat	groat	moat
mote	note	oat	quote
rote	smote	stoat	throat
tote	vote	wrote	afloat
anecdote	antidote	assymptote	connote
devote	lifeboat	misquote	outvote
petticoat	promote	remote	table d'hote

OATH, OTH

both	growth	loath	oath
quoth	sloth	troth	Arbroath

OATHE

clothe	loathe	betroth

OAX

coax	hoax

(And pluralize OAK, OKE, as in "oaks," "jokes.")

OB, OAB

blob	bob	Bob	cob
dob	fob	gob	hob
job	knob	lob	mob
nob	quab	rob	snob
sob	swab	throb	yob
cabob	demob	hobnob	nabob
thingumbob			

OBE

globe	Job	lobe	probe
robe	Anglophobe	conglobe	disrobe
enrobe	Francophobe		

OCK

block	bock	brock	chock
clock	cock	crock	dock
flock	frock	hock	hough
Jock	knock	Knocke	loch
lock	lough	mock	pock
roc	rock	shock	smock
sock	stock	padlock	pibroch
hollyhock	Jabberwock	laughing-stock	shamrock
stumbling-block	weathercock		

OCT

concoct   decoct

(*And preterites of* OCK, *as in* "locked," "padlocked," *etc.*)

OD

clod	cod	God	hod
nod	odd	plod	pod
prod	quad	quod	rod
shod	sod	tod	trod
wad	demigod	period	untrod

ODGE

bodge	dodge	hodge	lodge
podge	splodge	stodge	dislodge
hodge-podge			

OE (*see* O)

OFF

cough	doff	off	scoff
shroff	"soph"	toff	trough

OFT

croft	loft	oft	soft
aloft			

(*And preterites of verbs in* OFF.)

OG, OGUE

bog	clog	cog	dog
flog	fog	frog	gog
grog	hog	jog	log
prog	shog	stog	agog
analogue	apologue	catalogue	decalogue
demagogue	dialogue	duologue	epilogue
incog	monologue	pedagogue	synagogue

OGUE (*long*)

brogue	rogue	vogue	prorogue

OICE

Boyce	choice	Joyce	voice
invoice	rejoice	Rolls-Royce	

OID

Boyd	Floyd	Lloyd	void
alkaloid	asteroid	avoid	devoid
negroid	paraboloid	rhomboid	celluloid

(*And preterites of verbs in* OY, *as* "*destroyed.*")

OIL

boil	Boyle	broil	coil
Doyle	foil	moil	oil
roil	soil	spoil	toil
despoil	embroil	gumboil	Lough Foyle
parboil	turmoil		

(*Compare* OYAL.)

OIN, OYNE

Boyne	coign	coin	foin
groin	groyne	join	loin
quoin	adjoin	benzoin	conjoin

| disjoin | enjoin | purloin | rejoin |
| sainfoin | sirloin | subjoin | |

OINT

joint	oint	point	anoint
appoint	aroint	conjoint	counterpoint
disappoint	disjoint	West Point	

OISE, OYS

| froise | noise | poise | Troyes |
| avoirdupois | counterpoise | equipoise | |

(And add "s" to nouns and verbs in OY.)

OIST

| foist | hoist | joist | moist |
| voiced | invoiced | rejoiced | |

OIT

| doit | quoit | adroit | dacoit |
| Detroit | exploit | introit | |

OKE (*see* OAK)

OL, OLL (*both short*)

"coll."	doll	loll	Moll
poll	Sol	alcohol	capitol
extol	parasol	vitriol	

OL, OLL (*long*), OLE (*see* OAL)

OLD

bold	cold	fold	gold
hold	mold	old	scold
sold	told	wold	behold

cuckold	enfold	foretold	freehold
manifold	marigold	unfold	untold
uphold	withhold		

(*And see* OAL *for preterites of* OAL, OLE, OLL *and* OWL.)

OLK (*as in "folk," see* OAK)

OLT

bolt	colt	dolt	jolt
molt	poult	volt	revolt
thunderbolt			

OLVE

| solve | absolve | dissolve | evolve |
| involve | resolve | revolve | |

OM

bomb	from	pom	"Prom"
rhom	Somme	Tom	aplomb
pom-pom	tom-tom		

OMP

| comp | pomp | romp | swamp |

OMPT

| prompt | romped | swamped | |

ON

Bonn	con	don	gone
John	non	on	"scone" (*Scotch*)
shone	swan	wan	yon
anon	begone	bon-bon	bon-ton
bygone	Canton	Ceylon	dies-non
hereon	Marathon	Narbonne	sine qua non
thereon	thereupon	upon	

(*Compare* UN *for words of three syllables ending in* ON *as in "champion."*)

ONCE, ONSE

| nonce | ponce | sconce | ensconce |
| response | | | |

(*For rhymes to "once," see* UNCE.)

61

OND, ONNED

blond	bond	fond	frond
pond	wand	yond	abscond
beyond	correspond	co-respond	despond
diamond	respond	vagabond	demi-monde

(And preterites of verbs in ON, *as in "conned.")*

ONE (*short as in "one," see* UN)
ONE (*long, as in "tone," see* OAN)

ONG

gong	long	prong	song
strong	thong	throng	tong
wrong	along	belong	ding-dong
diphthong	Hong Kong	oblong	ping-pong
prolong	overlong		

ONGUE (*see* UNG)

ONK

bonk	conk	honk	plonk

(For "Bronx," add "s" to above.)

ONT (*short*)

font	want

ONT (*long*)

don't	wont	won't

ONZE

bonze	bronze	"onze" (*French*)

(And add "s" to words in ON, *as in "cons.")*

OO (*see* EW)   OOD (*as in "blood," see* UD)

OOD (*as in "hood"*)

could	good	hood	should
stood	wood	would	babyhood
brotherhood	childhood	fatherhood	Goodwood
hardihood	Hollywood	likelihood	livelihood
misunderstood	motherhood	neighborhood	understood
widowhood	withstood		

OOD (*as in "food"*), EUD, EWED, UDE

brood	Bude	crude	dude
feud	food	lewd	mood
nude	prude	rood	rude
shrewd	snood	you'd	alacritude
allude	altitude	amplitude	aptitude
assuetude	attitude	beatitude	certitude
collude	conclude	consuetude	crassitude
decrepitude	delude	denude	desuetude
detrude	disquietude	dissimilitude	elude
exactitude	exclude	extrude	exude
finitude	fortitude	gratitude	habitude
Hollyrood	illude	inaptitude	incertitude
include	ineptitude	infinitude	ingratitude
interlude	intrude	lassitude	latitude
longitude	magnitude	mansuetude	multitude
necessitude	obtrude	occlude	parvitude
platitude	plenitude	preclude	prelude
promptitude	protrude	pulchritude	quietude
rectitude	sanctitude	seclude	serenitude
servitude	similitude	solicitude	solitude

(See under EW *for preterites of many verbs in* EW, OO, *and* UE; *thus "hewed," "booed," "subdued.")*

OOF

hoof	oof	pouf	proof
roof	spoof	woof	aloof
behoof	disproof	reproof	

OOK

book	brook	cook	crook
hook	look	nook	took
shook	spook	took	"amuck"
betook	"Canuck"	forsook	mistook
nainsook	overlook	overtook	undertook

OOL, ULE (*when pronounced* OOL)

cool	fool	ghoul	Goole
pool	Poole	rule	school
spool	stool	tool	tulle
who'll	befool	misrule	overrule
sporrule	Stamboul		

(*Compare* ULE, *with diphthong, as in* "*mule.*" *Compare, also,* UEL *in two-syllable rhymes as in* "*fuel.*")

OOL (*as in* "*wool,*" *see* UL)

OOM, UME (*when pronounced* OOM)

bloom	boom	broom	brougham
coomb	coombe	doom	flume
gloom	groom	loom	plume
rheum	room	spoom	tomb
whom	womb	zoom	Batoum
beplume	dining-room	drawing-room	elbow-room
entomb	Ezroum	hecatomb	Khartoum
sitting-room			

(*Compare* UME *with diphthong, as in* "*fume.*")

OON, UNE (*when pronounced* OON)

boon	coon	croon	loon
lune	Lune	moon	poon
prune	rune	screwn	shoon
soon	spoon	strewn	swoon
Troon	afternoon	baboon	balloon
bassoon	bestrewn	buffoon	cartoon
cocoon	doubloon	dragoon	Dunoon
eftsoon	eschewn	festoon	galloon
harpoon	honeymoon	jejune	lagoon
lampoon	macaroon	maroon	monsoon
musketoon	octoroon	platoon	poltroon
pontoon	quadroon	racoon	Rangoon
rigadoon	shalloon	simoon	typhoon

(*Compare* UNE *with diphthong, as in* "*tune.*")

OOP, OUP

coop	croup	droop	group
hoop	loop	poop	scoop
sloop	snoop	soup	stoop

stoup	swoop	"goop"	troop
troupe	whoop	nincompoop	recoup

(*Compare* UPE.)

OOR

boor	floor	moor	poor
Ruhr	spoor	tour	you're
amour	blackamoor	contour	detour
paramour			

(*Compare* URE. *Also* EWER *in two-syllable rhymes. For rhymes to "door," see* OAR.)

OOSE (*short*), UCE, UICE (*when pronounced OOSE, short*)

Bruce	goose	juice	loose
moose	noose	sluice	spruce
truce	abstruse	occluse	recluse
unloose	induce	introduce	

(*Compare* UCE *and* USE *with diphthong, as in "puce" and "diffuse."*)

OOSE (*long*), OOZE, UES

booze	bruise	choose	cruise
lose	Ouse	ooze	ruse
trews	whose	who's	caboose
enthuse	papoose	recluse	peruse
vamoose			

(*Compare* USE, *as in "fuse," and see* EW, IEU, UE *and* OO *for plurals of nouns and third person singular of verbs, as in "pews," "adieus," "hues," etc.*)

OOST, UCED, USED (*sharp*)

boost	joust	juiced	loosed
noosed	roost	sluiced	spruced
used	adduced	conduced	deduced
educed	induced	produced	reduced
reproduced	seduced	subduced	superinduced

OOT (*short*)

foot	put	soot

OOT (long), UTE (when pronounced OOT)

boot	bruit	brute	coot
flute	fruit	hoot	jute
loot	moot	root	route
shoot	skoot	toot	adjute
cheroot	galloot	overshoot	parachute
recruit	uproot	waterchute	

(*Compare* UTE *with diphthong, as in* "cute," "newt," *etc.*)

OOTH (short), UTH

ruth	Ruth	sooth	"strewth"
tooth	truth	youth	Duluth
forsooth	uncouth	untruth	vermouth

OOTH (long)

booth	smooth	soothe

OOVE

groove	hoove	move	prove
you've	approve	disprove	improve
remove	reprove	disapprove	

OOZE (see OOSE)

OP

chop	cop	crop	drop
flop	fop	hop	lop
mop	plop	pop	prop
shop	slop	sop	stop
strop	swap	top	whop
wop	atop		

OPE, OAP

cope	dope	grope	hope
lope	mope	nope	ope
pope	rope	scope	slope

soap	tope	trope	antelope
antipope	bioscope	Good Hope	envelope
gyroscope	helioscope	heliotrope	horoscope
interlope	kaleidoscope	microscope	misanthrope
periscope	polyscope	stethoscope	telescope

OPSE, OPS

copse   (*And extend* OP)

OPT

Copt   adopt

(*And preterites of verbs in* OP.)

OR

for	lor'	nor	or
Thor	tor	war	abhor
ambassador	ancestor	anterior	apparitor
auditor	bachelor	chancellor	competitor
compositor	conqueror	conspirator	contributor
corridor	councillor	counselor	creditor
cuspidor	editor	emperor	escritoire
excelsior	executor	expositor	exterior
furore	governor	inferior	inheritor
inquisitor	interior	junior	lessor
louis d'or	matador	memoir	metaphor
meteor	minotaur	mortgagor	orator
picador	posterior	progenitor	reservoir
rouge-et-noir	Salvador	seignior	senator
señor	servitor	solicitor	superior
vice-chancellor	warrior		

(*Compare* OAR.)

ORCE, ORSE, OARSE, OURCE

coarse	corse	course	force
gorse	hawse	hoarse	horse
morse	Norse	sauce	source
torse	concourse	discourse	divorce
endorse	enforce	perforce	recourse
remorse	resource	intercourse	unhorse

ORCH

porch	scorch	torch	debauch

ORD (*as in* "cord," *see* OARD) ORD (*as in* "word," *see* EARD)

ORGE

forge	George	gorge	disgorge
engorge	regorge	overgorge	

ORK

cork	fork	pork	stork
torque	York	New York	

(*Compare* ALK *and* AUK.)

ORLD (*see* EARLED)

ORM

form	norm	storm	swarm
warm	conform	chloroform	cruciform
cuneiform	deform	Great Orme	inform
iodoform	misinform	multiform	perform
reform	transform	thunderstorm	uniform
vermiform			

ORN, ORNE

born	borne	corn	horn
lorn	morn	scorn	shorn
sorn	sworn	thorn	torn
warn	worn	acorn	adorn
barley-corn	Cape Horn	Capricorn	forborne
forlorn	forsworn	Leghorn	lovelorn
peppercorn	suborn	unicorn	

(*Compare* OURN *and* AWN.)

ORP

dorp	thorp	warp

ORSE (*see* ORCE)

ORT

court	fort	forte	mort
ort	port	porte	quart
short	snort	sort	sport
swart	thwart	tort	wart
cavort	cohort	comport	consort
contort	deport	disport	distort
escort	exhort	export	extort
import	purport	rapport	report
resort	support	transport	misreport

(*Compare* AUT, AUGHT *and* OUGHT.)

ORTH

forth	fourth	north	Porth
swarth	henceforth	thenceforth	

OSE (*short*)

dose	gross	jocose	morose

OSE (*long*)

chose	close	clothes	does (*pl. of "doe"*)
doze	froze	gloze	hose
nose	pose	prose	"pros"
rose	Rose	those	arose
banjos	compose	depose	depots
disclose	discompose	dispose	expose
foreclose	indispose	interpose	Montrose
redose	oppose	predispose	presuppose
recompose	repose	suppose	transpose
tuberose	unclose		

(*For more than sixty other good rhymes, see plurals of nouns and third person singulars of verbs in* O, OW *and* OE.)

OSH (*as in "wash," see* ASH)

OSS

boss	cross	doss	dross
floss	fosse	gloss	"Goss" (*china*)
joss	loss	moss	posse
Ross	toss	across	emboss
albatross	cerebos	reredos	

69

OST

cost	frost	lost	wast
accost	exhaust	holocaust	pentecost

(And preterites of OS, *as in "bossed.")*

OST (*as in "most," see* OAST)

OT, OTTE

blot	clot	cot	dot
got	grot	hot	jot
knot	lot	mot	not
plot	pot	rot	Scot
shot	slot	snot	sot
spot	squat	swat	swot
tot	trot	what	wot
yacht	Aldershot	aliquot	allot
apricot	bergamot	boycott	camelot
chariot	cocotte	compatriot	counterplot
echalot	forgot	gallipot	garotte
gavotte	idiot	patriot	polyglot
unbegot			

OTCH

blotch	botch	crotch	notch
potch	Scotch	watch	hop-scotch
hotch-potch			

OTE (*see* OAT)   OTH (*long, see* OATH)

OTH (*short*)

broth	cloth	froth	Goth
moth	wroth	behemoth	

OUCH

couch	crouch	grouch	pouch
slouch	vouch	avouch	scaramouch

OUCH (*soft*)

mouch   debouch

OUD, OWD

cloud	crowd	dowd	loud
proud	shroud	Stroud	aloud

(*And preterites of* OW, *as in "bowed."*)

OUGH (*see* O, OCK, OFF, OW, UF) OUGHT (*see* AUGHT)

OUL (*see* OAL)   OULD (*see* OLD)

OUNCE

bounce	flounce	frounce	ounce
pounce	trounce	announce	denounce
pronounce	renounce		

OUND, OWNED

bound	found	ground	hound
mound	pound	round	sound
wound	abound	aground	around
astound	compound	confound	dumfound
expound	inbound	outbound	profound
propound	rebound	redound	resound
surround	unbound	unsound	underground

(*And preterites and adjectives of words in* OWN, *as in "clowned" and "renowned."*)

OUND (*as in "wound," an injury. See preterites of verbs in OON, as in "crooned"*)

OUNGE

lounge   scrounge

71

OUNT

count	fount	mount	account
amount	discount	dismount	miscount
paramount	recount	remount	surmount
tantamount			

OUP (see OOP)

OUR

dour	flour	hour	our
scour	sour	devour	

(*Compare* OWER *in two-syllable rhymes.*)

OURD

gourd	Lourdes	moored

(*And extend* OUR *as in "toured."*)

OURN

bourn	mourn

(*Compare* ORN.)

OURSE (see ORCE)   OUS (see US)

OUS (short)

chouse	dowse	grouse	house
louse	mouse	nous	souse
carouse (*noun*)	charnel-house	custom-house	Strauss

OUSE (long)

drowse	blouse	blowze	browse
house (*verb*)	rouse	spouse	touse
carouse (*verb*)	espouse	unhouse	uprouse

(*And plurals of nouns and third person singulars of verbs
in* OW *and* OUGH, *as in "brows," "bows," "boughs"
and "ploughs."*)

OUT

bout	clout	doubt	drought
flout	gout	grout	knout

lout	nowt	out	owt
pout	rout	scout	shout
snout	spout	sprout	stout
tout	trout	about	devout
misdoubt	redoubt	roundabout	sauerkraut
throughout	waterspout	without	

OUTH

| drouth | Louth | mouth | south |

(*For rhymes to "youth," see* OOTH.)

OVE (*short*)

| dove | glove | love | shove |
| above | turtledove | | |

OVE (*long*)

clove	cove	drove	grove
hove	Hove	Jove	rove
stove	strove	throve	trove
wove	alcove	behove	interwove
treasure-trove			

(OVE, *as in "proove," see* OOVE.)

OW (*as in "cow"*), OUGH

bough	bow	brow	chow
cow	dhow	frau	how
now	plough	prow	row
scow	slough	Slough	sow
thou	trow	wow	vow
allow	avow	bow-wow	disallow
disendow	endow	enow	Foochow
kow-tow	somehow		

OW (*as in "know," see* O)

OWL, OUL

cowl	foul	fowl	ghoul (*also pro-*
growl	jowl	owl	*nounced "gool"*)
prowl	scowl	befoul	

(*Compare* OWELL *in two-syllable rhymes.*)

OWN

brown	clown	crown	down
drown	frown	gown	noun
town	Cape Town	eiderdown	embrown
pronoun	renown	upside down	

OX, OCKS

box	"chocs."	cox	fox
ox	phlox	pox	approx.
equinox	heterodox	orthodox	paradox

(And plurals of nouns and third person singulars of verbs in OCK as in "frocks," "mocks.")

OY

boy	buoy	cloy	coy
gloy	hoy	joy	oi!
soy	toy	troy	Troy
alloy	Amoy	annoy	convoy
decoy	destroy	employ	enjoy
envoy	overjoy	pomeroy	Savoy
saveloy	sepoy	yoi-yoi!	

UB

blub	bub	chub	club
cub	drub	dub	grub
hub	pub	rub	scrub
shrub	snub	stub	sub
tub	hubbub	sillabub	Beelzebub

UBE

cube	"rube"	tube	jujube

UCE, USE

duce	juice	puce	use (*noun*)
abuse (*noun*)	conduce	deduce	diffuse
educe	excuse (*noun*)	introduce	obtuse
produce	reduce	refuse (*noun*)	seduce
traduce	abstruse		

(Compare OOSE, hard, and, under same heading, UCE, without "u" sound, as in "truce.")

74

UCH, UTCH

clutch	crutch	Dutch	hutch
much	such	touch	inasmuch
insomuch	overmuch	retouch	

UCK

buck	chuck	cluck	duck
luck	muck	pluck	puck
ruck	shuck	struck	suck
truck	tuck	thunderstruck	

UCT, UCKED

duct	abduct	aqueduct	conduct (*verb*)
deduct	induct	instruct	misconduct
obstruct	usufruct	viaduct	

(*And preterites of verbs in* UCK, *as in* "mucked.")

UD

blood	bud	cud	dud
flood	mud	rudd	scud
spud	stud	sud	thud

UDE (*see* OOD *long*)

UDGE

budge	drudge	fudge	grudge
judge	nudge	sludge	smudge
snudge	trudge	adjudge	misjudge
prejudge			

UE (*see* EW)

UFT

cruft	tuft

(*And past participles of verbs in* UF.)

UFF

bluff	buff	chough	chuff
clough	cuff	duff	fluff
Gough	gruff	guff	huff
luff	muff	puff	rough

ruff	scruff	slough	snuff
sough	stuff	tough	enough
rebuff			

UISE (*see* OOSE *long*)   UIT (*see* OOT *long*)

UG

bug	chug	dug	drug
hug	jug	lug	mug
plug	pug	rug	shrug
slug	smug	snug	tug

UKE

duke	fluke	Luke	puke
archduke	mameluke	peruke	rebuke

UL, ULL (*as in "bull"*)

bull	full	pull	wool
beautiful	bountiful	dutiful	fanciful
merciful	plentiful	powerful	sorrowful
wonderful	worshipful		

UL, ULL (*as in "dull"*)

cull	dull	gull	hull
Hull	lull	mull	null
scull	skull	trull	annul
bulbul	disannul	numskull	seagull

ULE (*with "u" sounded*)

mule	pule	tuhl	Yule
reticule	ridicule	vestibule	

(*Compare* OOL, *and, under same heading,* ULE, *without "u" sound, as in "rule." Also* UEL *in two-syllable rhymes.*)

ULGE

bulge	divulge	indulge	promulge

ULK

bulk	hulk	pulque	skulk
sulk			

ULP

gulp	pulp	sculp

ULSE

mulse	pulse	appulse	convulse
expulse	impulse	insulse	repulse

ULT

cult	ult	adult	catapult
consult	difficult	exult	insult
occult	result	tumult	

UM, BRUM

Brum	bum	chum	come
crumb	drum	dumb	glum
gum	hum	mum	mumm
numb	plum	plumb	rum
scrum	scum	slum	some
strum	sum	swum	thrum
thumb	become	benumb	

And false rhymes, as follows:

adventuresome	auditorium	burdensome	compendium
cranium	crematorium	cumbersome	delirium
effluvium	emporium	enconium	opithalamium
equilibrium	exordium	fee-fo-fum	frolicsome
gymnasium	harmonium	humdrum	humoursome
laudanum	magnesium	medium	mettlesome
millennium	minimum	misbecome	modicum
odium	opium	opprobium	palladium
pandemonium	pendulum	petroleum	premium
quarrelsome	residium	sanitorium	sensorium
solatium	spectrum	symposium	troublesome
tympanium	wearisome		

UME

fume	plume	spume	assume
consume	exhume	Fiume	illume
perfume	presume	relume	resume
reassume			

(Compare OOM.)

UMP

bump	chump	clump	dump
frump	grump	gump	hump
jump	lump	mump	plump
pump	rump	slump	stump
sump	thump	trump	

UN

bun	done	dun	fun
gun	Hun	none	nun
one	pun	run	shun
son	spun	stun	sun
ton	tun	won	anyone
begun	everyone	forerun	overdone
overrun	undone		

(*And about* 100 *false rhymes of words of three syllables and over ending in* ON *and* TON, *such as "criterion" and "skeleton."*)

UNCE

bunce	dunce	once

UNCH

brunch	bunch	crunch	hunch
lunch	munch	punch	scrunch

UNCT, UNKED

bunked	funked	adjunct	defunct
debunked			

UND

bund	fund	fecund	jocund
moribund	refund	rotund	rubicund
verecund			

(*And preterites of verbs in* UN *as in "punned."*)

UNE

dune	hewn	June	tune
viewn	commune	immune	importune

78

| impugn | inopportune | jejune | opportune |
| pursuen | subduen | triune | |

(*Compare* OON, *and, under same heading,* UNE *with "u" not pronounced, as in "prune."*)

UNG

bung	clung	dung	flung
hung	lung	rung	slung
sprung	strung	stung	sung
swung	tongue	wrung	young
among	Shantung	unhung	unsung

UNGE

| lunge | plunge | sponge | axunge |
| expunge . | | | |

UNK

bunk	chunk	drunk	funk
hunk	junk	monk	plunk
punk	shrunk	skunk	slunk
spunk	stunk	sunk	trunk
quidnunc			

UNT

blunt	brunt	bunt	front
grunt	hunt	lunt	punt
runt	shunt	stunt	affront
confront			

UP

| crup | cup | pup | sup |
| tup | up | hiccough | |

UPE

| drupe | dupe |

(*Compare* OOP.)

UPT

| abrupt | corrupt | disrupt |

(*And preterites of verbs in* UP, *as in "cupped."*)

UR (*see* ER)   URB (*see* ERB)   URD (*see* EARD)

cure	dure	lure	Muir
pure	sure	abjure	adjure
conjure	cocksure	ensure	immure
insure	obscure	nomenclature	

(*Compare* OOR, *also* EWER *in two-syllable rhymes.*)

URF (*see* ERF)   URGE (*see* ERGE)

URK (*see* ERK)   URL (*see* EARL)

URN (*see* EARN)   URP (*see* IRP)

URSE (*see* ERCE)   URST (*see* IRST)

URT (*see* ERT)   URVE (*see* ERVE)

URZE

furze   thyrse

(*And add "s" to words in* ER, IR *and* UR.)

US, USS

bus	buss	cuss	fuss
Gus	plus	pus	thus
truss	us	discuss	nonplus

(*And nearly* 300 *false rhymes in words of three syllables and over, which end in* US *and* OUS. *Thus "sarcophagus" and "impetuous."*)

USE (*short, see* UCE)

USE (*long*)

fuse	muse	use (*verb*)	abuse
accuse	amuse	confuse	contuse
diffuse	disabuse	disuse	enthuse
excuse	hypotenuse	peruse	Syracuse
transfuse			

(*See* EW, IFU, UE *and* OO *for plurals of nouns and third person singulars of verbs, as in "pews," "adieus," "blues" and "moos." Compare* OOSE *and, under same heading,* USE *when "u" is not sounded, as in "peruse."*)

USH (*as in "bush"*)

bush	"cush"	push	ambush
	(*billiards*)		

USH (*as in "blush"*)

blush	brush	crush	flush
frush	gush	hush	lush
mush	plush	rush	slush
thrush	tush		

USK

rusk	dusk	husk	musk
busk	tusk	Usk	

UST

bust	crust	dost	dust
gust	just	lust	must
rust	thrust	trust	adjust
august	disgust	distrust	entrust
incrust	mistrust	robust	unjust

(*And preterites in* USS, *as in "fussed."*)

UT, UTT

but	butt	crut	cut
glut	gut	hut	jut
Kut	mutt	nut	phut
putt	rut	scut	shut
slut	smut	strut	tut
abut	catgut	coconut	englut
gamut	halibut	occiput	rebut
waterbutt			

(*For rhymes to "put," see* OOT.)

UTE

Bute	"beaut"	chute	cute
jute	lute	mute	newt
suit	absolute	acute	arbute
argute	attribute	Canute	comminute
commute	compute	confute	constitute
contribute	depute	destitute	dilute

81

dispute	disrepute	dissolute	execute
impute	institute	irresolute	minute
parachute	persecute	pollute	prosecute
prostitute	pursuit	refute	repute
resolute	salute	substitute	transmute
volute			

(Compare OOT *and, under same heading,* UTE, *when "u" is not sounded, as in "flute.")*

UTH *(see* OOTH)

UX, UCKS

Bucks	crux	dux	flux
lux	conflux	efflux	influx
reflux			

(And plurals of nouns and third person singulars of verbs in UCK. *Thus "ducks," "mucks.")*

UZ

buzz	coz	does	doz.
muzz	Uz		

Y

aye	buy	by	bye
cry	die	dry	dye
eye	fie	fly	fry
guy	Guy	hi!	hie
high	I	lie	lye
my	nigh	pie	ply
pry	rye	Rye	shy
sigh	sky	Skye	sly
spry	spy	sty	thigh
thy	tie	try	vie
why	wry	Wye	alkali
ally	amplify	apply	awry
beatify	beautify	belie	candefy
certify	clarify	classify	comply
crucify	decry	defy	deify
descry	dignify	disqualify	diversify
dignify	dulcify	edify	espy
falsify	fortify	Frenchify	fructify
glorify	go-by	good-bye	gratify

82

hereby	harmonify	horrify	imply
indemnify	intensify	justify	labefy
lenify	liquefy	lullaby	magnify
modify	mollify	mortify	multiply
notify	nullify	occupy	ossify
outcry	outfly	outvie	pacify
personify	petrify	preoccupy	prophecy
prophesy	purify	putrefy	qualify
ramify	rarefy	ratify	rectify
rely	reply	rubefy	sanctify
satisfy	scarify	Shanghai	signify
simplify	solidify	specify	stupefy
supply	tabefy	terrify	testify
thereby	typify	unify	untie
verify	versify	villify	whereby

(There are more than 2,000 words ending in Y short—thus "necessity." But these make very poor rhymes and are hardly worth consideration.)

YLE (*see* ILE)   YME (*see* IME)

YMPH

lymph   nymph

YNX (*see* INX)   YP (*see* IP)

YRE (*see* IRE)   YST (*see* IST)

YTH (*see* ITH)   YTHE (*see* ITHE)

YVE (*see* IVE)   YX (*see* IX)

END OF ONE-SYLLABLE SECTION

PART II

TWO-SYLLABLE RHYMES

TWO-SYLLABLE RHYMES

ABARD
jabbered   scabbard   tabard

ABBER (*Extend* AB *for such words as* "*jabber*," *etc.*)

ABBLE
babble   dabble   drabble   gabble
rabble   scrabble   bedabble   bedrabble
(*For rhymes to* "*squabble*," *see* OBBLE.)

ABBOT
abbot   jabot   sabot

ABBEY, ABBY
abbey   flabby   shabby
(*And extend* AB *for such rhymes as* "*cabby*.")

ABEL (*see* ABLE)

ABID
rabid   tabid

ABIAN, ABION
fabian   gabion   Sabian   Arabian

ABIES
babies   gabies   Jabez   rabies
scabies

ABIT

habit	rabbit	cohabit	inhabit

ABLE, ABEL

Abel	able	babel	cable
fable	gabel	gable	label
Mabel	sable	stable	table
disable	enable	unable	unstable

ABOR, ABER

caber (*Scotch*)	labor	neighbor	saber
tabor	belabor		

ABY

baby	gaby	maybe

ACA

"bacca"	Dacca	paca	alpaca
malacca			

(*Compare* ACKER.)

ACENT, ASCENT

jacent	nascent	adjacent	complacent
complaisant	interjacent	renascent	subjacent

ACET (*see* ASSET)

ACIAL

glacial	racial	spatial	palatial

ACID

acid	flaccid	fracid	placid

ACIOUS, ATIOUS

gracious	spacious	audacious	bibacious
bulbaceous	capacious	cetaceous	contumacious
cretaceous	disputatious	edaceous	efficacious

fallacious	farinaceous	herbaceous	Horatius
Ignatius	incapacious	linguacious	loquacious
mendacious	minacious	mordacious	ostentatious
perspicacious	pertinacious	predaceous	procacious
pugnacious	rapacious	sagacious	salacious
saponaceous	sequacious	setaceous	tenacious
ungracious	veracious	vexatious	vivacious
voracious			

ACIS, ASIS

basis   glacis   oasis

    (*Compare plurals in* ACE.)

ACKAGE

package   trackage

ACKEN

blacken   bracken   slacken

ACKER, ACQUER

claquer   lacquer

    (*And extend* ACK *for* "*blacker,*" *etc.*)

ACKET

bracket   jacket   packet   plaquet
racket

ACKEY, ACKY

baccy   blackie   Jacky   lackey
quacky   tacky

    ACKLE (*Extend* AC *and* ACK *for* "*cackle,*" "*demoniacal,*"
      etc.)

    ACTER, ACTOR (*Extend* ACK *for* "*actor,*" "*exacter,*"
      etc.)

ACTIC

lactic   tactic   didactic   prophylactic

ACTILE

dactyle (*or dactyl*)   tactile   tractile

89

ACTION

action	faction	fraction	paction
taction	traction	abstraction	arefaction
attraction	benefaction	calefaction	co-action
compaction	contaction	contraction	counteraction
detraction	distraction	dissatisfaction	exaction
extraction	impaction	inaction	infaction
liquefaction	malefaction	petrifaction	protraction
putrefaction	rarefaction	reaction	refraction
retraction	retroaction	satisfaction	stupefaction
subaction	subtraction	transaction	

ACTIVE

active	tractive	abstractive	attractive
calefractive	distractive	inactive	petrifactive
protractive	purifactive	putrefactive	reactive
retractive	retroactive	stupefactive	

ACTRESS

actress	benefactress	detractress	malefactress

ACTURE

fracture	compacture	manufacture

ACY

Casey	Gracie	lacy	racy
Stracey			

ADAM

Adam	madam	macadam

ADDEN

bad'un	gladden	madden	sadden
Abaddon			

ADDER

adder	bladder	gadder	gladder
ladder	madder	padder	sadder

ADDEST, ADDIST

faddist	gladdest	maddest	saddest
sadist			

ADDLE

addle	faddle	paddle	raddle
saddle	spaddle	straddle	skedaddle

ADDOCK

Braddock	haddock	Maddock	paddock
shaddock			

ADDY

caddy	daddy	faddy	laddie
paddy			

ADEN, AIDEN

Aden	Haydn	laden	maiden
Sladen	overladen		

ADGER

badger	cadger

ADIENT

gradient	radiant

ADISH, ADDISH

baddish	caddish	gaddish	radish

ADIUM

radium	stadium	palladium

ADLE

cradle	ladle

ADO

dado	spado	bastinado	bravado
crusado	desperado	Mikado	passado
tornado			

(Most of the above words may be pronounced with the "a" long or short.)

ADRE

cadre	padre

ADY, ADI

Brady	cadi	cady	lady
maidie	O'Brady	Sadie	shady

AFFER, AFFIR, AUGHER

chaffer	gaffer	Jaffa	Kaffir
laugher	quaffer	photographer	cinematographer

AFFIC

graphic	"maffick"	traffic	cinematographic
paragraphic	phonographic	photographic	pornographic
seismographic	seraphic	telegraphic	

AFFLE

baffle	raffle	snaffle

AFFLED, AFFOLD

baffled	raffled	scaffold	snaffled

AFFY

café	chaffy	draffy	Taffy

AFTER

after	dafter	grafter	laughter
rafter	shafter	wafter	hereafter
thereinafter			

AGA, AGER (*hard*)

lager	saga

AGER, AJOR

gauger	major (*And extend* AGE *for "sager," etc.*)

AGGARD

blackguard	haggard	laggard	staggered
swaggered			

AGGER

dagger	sagger (*And extend* AG *for "bragger," etc.*)

AGGLE

draggle	gaggle	haggle	straggle
waggle	bedraggle		

AGGOT, AGATE

agate	Baggot	faggot	maggot

AGGY, AGGIE

Aggie	baggy	craggy	jaggy
knaggy	Maggie	quaggy	scraggy
shaggy	snaggy	swaggy	waggy

AGIC

magic	tragic	pelagic

AGILE

agile	fragile

AGO

dago	sago	Chicago	farrago
lumbago	Tobago	virago	

(*Most of the above words may be pronounced with either the broad "a" or the narrow.*) (*Compare* ARGO *as in* "cargo," *etc.*)

AGON

dragon	flagon	wagon

AGRANT

flagrant	fragrant	vagrant

AGSHIP

flagship	hagship

AIC

caique	algebraic	archaic	Hebraic
Judaic	mosaic	prosaic	

AIDEN (*see* ADEN)

AIETY, AITY

gaiety	laity

AILER

gaoler (*And extend* AIL *for "jailer," "sailor," etc.*)

AILIFF

bailiff   caliph

AILING

paling   grayling (*And extend* AIL *for "prevailing," etc.*)

AILMENT, ALMENT

(*Extend* AIL, ALE *for "ailment," "regalement," etc.*)

AILY, ALY

bailey	bailie	daily	Daly
gaily	greyly	maily	palely
scaly	shaly	snaily	stalely
vale (*Latin*)			

AIMENT, AYMENT

claimant	clamant	payment	raiment
displayment	defrayment	repayment	

AINFUL, ANEFUL

baneful	gainful	painful	disdainful

AINTER

(*Extend* AINT *for "quainter," etc.*)

AINTLY

faintly   quaintly   saintly

AINY

brainy	drainy	grainy	rainy
Slaney	veiny	"champagney"	Delaney

AIRY, ARY

airy	chary	dairy	eyrie
fairy	Gary	hairy	Mary
nary	prairie	snary	vary
wary	canary	Tipperary	vagary

(*And many false rhymes, such as "ordinary," etc.*)

AISER (*see* AZOR)   AISIN (*see* AZEN)   AISY (*see* AZY)

AITEN, ATAN

Dayton   Leyton   Satan   straighten
straiten

AITER (*see* ATER)

AITHFUL

faithful   scatheful

AITRESS

creatress   traitress   waitress

AJOR (*see* AGER)

AKEN, ACON

bacon   (*And extend* AKE *for* "*awaken,*" *etc.*)

AKER, ACRE

acher   acre   baker   fakir
nacre   Quaker   Straker   Long Acre
wiseacre

(*And extend* AKE, AIK *for* "*waker,*" "*breaker*" *and other
rhymes.*)

AKO, ACCO

Jacko   shako   tobacco

AKY

achy   Blaikie   braky   flaky
quaky   shaky   snaky

ALA

Bala   gala   Scala   cicala
                (*Compare* ARLER)

ALACE, ALLOUS

callous   Dallas   palace   Pallas
phallus   (*Compare* ALICE)

95

ALAD, ALLAD

ballad   salad

ALANCE

balance   valance

ALATE, ALLET, ALLOT

ballot   mallet   palate   pallet
shallot   valet

ALDER

alder   balder   Calder   scalder

ALDING

balding   scalding   Spalding

ALIA

dahlia   failure   Thalia   Australia
interalia   regalia   Westphalia

ALIAN, ALIEN, ALION

alien   Thalian   Australian   bacchanalian
episcopalian   Pygmalion   tatterdemalion   sesquipedalian
Westphalian

ALICE

Alice   chalice   malice   (*Compare* ALACE.)

ALID, ALLIED

calid   dallied   pallid   rallied
sallied   tallied   valid   invalid (*adj.*)

ALIPH (*see* AILIFF)

ALKER, AWKER, ORKER (*extend* ALK, AWK, ORK)

ALLANT

gallant   talent

ALLER, AWLER (*extend* ALL, AWL)   ALLET (*see* ALATE)

ALLIC

Alec	Gallic	phallic	medallic
metallic	vandallic		

ALLION

galleon	scallion	stallion	battalion
medallion	rapscallion		

ALLISH

Dawlish	Gaulish	smallish	tallish

ALLON

Alan	Allen	gallon	talon

ALLOP

gallop	jalap	Salop	shallop
escallop			

ALLOP (*broad*), OLLOP

dollop	gollop	scallop	wallop
trollop			

ALLOR

pallor	valour

ALLOW

aloe	callow	fallow	hallo
mallow	Mallow	sallow	shallow
tallow	(*Add "s" to the above for "gallows."*)		

ALLY

alley	ballet	bally	Calais
chalet	dally	galley	pally
rally	sally	Sally	tally
valley	reveille	shilly-shally	

(*A number of false rhymes by wrongly accentuating last two syllables of certain adverbs, such as "principally."*)

97

ALMER

calmer	palmer	embalmer	salaamer

(*Compare* AMA *and* ARMER.)

ALMEST, ALMIST

calmest	palmist	embalmist	psalmist

(*Compare* ARMEST.)

ALMON (*see* AMMON)   ALMY (*see* ARMY)

ALTAR, ALTER, AULTER

altar	alter	falter	halter
Malta	palter	psalter	salter
vaulter	Walter	assaulter	defaulter
drysalter	Gibraltar		

ALTRY

paltry	psaltery	drysaltery

ALTY, AULTY

faulty	malty	salty	vaulty

AMA

Brahma	drama	lama	llama
Rama	Alabama	melodrama	pajama
Yokohama			

(*Compare* ALMER *and* ARMER.)

AMBEAU, AMBO

crambo	flambeau	Sambo	zambo

AMBER

amber	camber	clamber	tambour
timbre			

AMBIT

ambit	gambit

AMBLE

amble
gambol
shamble

bramble
ramble
wamble

Campbell
scamble
preamble

gamble
scramble

AMBO (*see* AMBEAU)

AMEFUL

blameful

shameful

AMEL

camel

trammel

enamel

AMINE

famine
examine

gamin
cross-examine

stamen

stamin

AMLET

camlet

hamlet

Hamlet

samlet

AMMAR, AMMER, AMOR

clamor
hammer

dammar
stammer

gammer
yammer

glamor

(*And extend* AM *for* "crammer," *etc.*)

AMMON, ALMON

gammon

mammon

salmon

backgammon

AMMY

clammy
hammy
tammy

damme
jammy
whammy

drammie
mammy

gammy
Sammy

99

AMPER

camper	champer	clamper	cramper
damper	hamper	pamper	ramper
scamper	stamper	tamper	tramper
vamper	decamper		

AMPLE

ample	sample	trample	example

AMPUS

campus	grampus	pampas	wampus

AMOUS, AMUS

amous	ramous	squamous	mandamus

ANA

lana	banana	bandana	Havǎna
iguana	Indiana	Juliana	Louisiana
Montana	Nirvana		

ANCER, ANSWER

answer	cancer	dancer	lancer
prancer	advancer	geomancer	necromancer
romancer			

ANCET, ANSIT

lancet	transit	Narragansett

ANCID

fancied	rancid

ANCHOR, ANCOUR (*see* ANKER)

ANCY

fancy	Nancy	aeromancy	arithomancy
cheiromancy	geomancy	hesitancy	lithomancy
necromancy	occupancy	onomancy	rhabdomancy
romancy	termagancy	vagrancy	

ANDAL (*see* ANDLE)

ANDAM, ANDEM, ANDOM

granddam	random	tandem	memorandum
nil desperandum			

ANDANT, ANDENT

candent	commandant	demandant

ANDATE, ANDIT

bandit	mandate	pandit

ANDA, ANDER, ANDOUR

blander	brander	candour	dander
gander	glander	grander	hander
panda	pander	slander	stander
Alexander	commander	coriander	demander
expander	gerrymander	Leander	Lysander
meander	oleander	philander	pomander
propaganda	reprimander	salamander	Uganda

ANDID, ANDED

candid   (*And extend* AND *for "sanded," etc.*)
   (*Compare* ANDIED.)

ANDIED

bandied	brandied	candid	candied

ANDIER, ANDEUR

bandier	candier	grandeur	handier
sandier			

ANDISH

blandish   brandish   standish   outlandish

ANDIT (*see* ANDATE)

ANDLE, ANDAL

candle	dandle	Handel	handle
Randall	sandal	scandal	vandal
Coromandel			

ANDLER

chandler   dandler   handler   tallow-chandler

ANDOM (*see* ANDAM)   ANDOUR (*see* ANDER)

ANDREL, ANDRIL

band-drill   hand-drill   mandrel   mandrill

ANDSOME (*see* ANSOM)   ANDUM (*see* ANDAM)

ANDY

Andy	bandy	brandy	candy
dandy	Gandhi	handy	Kandy
randy	sandy	Sandy	shandy
organdie	unhandy		

ANEL, ANIL, ANNEL

anil	cannel	channel	flannel
panel	scrannel	empanel	

ANELY, AINLY (*extend* AIN, ANE) ANER, AINER (*extend* AIN, ANE)

ANET, ANNET, ANITE

gannet	granite	Janet	planet
Thanet	pomegranate		

ANGER (*hard "g"*)

anger	banger	Bangor	clangor
ganger	hanger	languor	slanger
haranguer			

ANGER (*soft "g"*)

changer	danger	manger	ranger
stranger	arranger	endanger	Grainger

ANGLE

angle	bangle	dangle	rangle
jangle	mangle	spangle	strangle
tangle	twangle	wangle	wrangle
disentangle	entangle	triangle	untangle

ANGLED, ANGLER, ANGLING (*adapt above*)

ANGO

mango	tango	contango	fandango

ANGUISH

anguish	languish

ANIC, ANNIC

Alnwick	panic	stannic	tannic
botanic	Britannic	diaphanic	galvanic
Germanic	mechanic	oceanic	organic
Romanic	Satanic	talismanic	titanic
tyrannic	volcanic		

ANIEL, ANNUAL

annual	Daniel	manual	spaniel
Nathaniel			

ANISH, ANNISH

banish	clannish	Danish	mannish
planish	Spanish	vanish	

ANATE (*see* ANET)

ANKARD, ANKERED, ANCHORED

anchored   bankered   cankered   hankered
tankard

ANKER, ANCHOR, ANCOUR

anchor   Bianca   canker   rancor
(And extend ANK *for "banker," etc.)*

ANKLE   ANKLY *(extend* ANK*)*

ankle   rankle

ANKY

Frankie   hankey   thankee   Yankee
(Extend ANK *for "swanky," etc.)*

ANLY

Cranleigh   Hanley   manly   Stanley

ANNA, ANNAH

anna   Anna   Hannah   manna
Havana   hosannah   Savannah   Susannah
(Compare ANA *and* ANNER.)

ANNER, ANOR

banner   canner   manner   manor
spanner   tanner
(And extend AN *for "fanner," etc.)*

ANNEX

annex   panics   galvanics   mechanics

ANNON

cannon   Shannon   Clackmannan

ANON

anon   canon

ANNY

Annie	branny	canny	cranny
Fanny	granny	mannie	nanny
zany			

ANSACK

Anzac   ransack

ANSION

mansion   scansion   stanchion   expansion

ANSOM, ANDSOME

handsome   hansom   ransom   transom

ANSWER (*see* ANCER)

ANSY, ANTAM, ANTOM

pansy   tansy   bantam   phantom

ANTE, ANTI, ANTY

ante	anti	chanty	chianti
Dante	scanty	shanty	andante
Bacchante	dilettante		

ANTEL (*see* ANTLE)

ANTER

banter	canter	cantor	chanter
granter	grantor	panter	planter
ranter	scanter	decanter	descanter
displanter	enchanter	implanter	recanter
supplanter	transplanter	"Atlanta"	

ANTHER

anther   panther

ANTIC

| antic | frantic | Atlantic | corybantic |
| gigantic | pedantic | romantic | sycophantic |

ANTILE

pantile   infantile

ANTLE

cantle   mantel   mantle   dismantle

ANTLER

antler   mantler   pantler   dismantler

ANTLING

bantling   mantling   scantling   dismantling

ANTO, ANTEAU

canto   panto   esperanto   Lepanto
portmanteau

ANTOM (*see* ANTAM)   ANTY (*see* ANTE)

ANTRY

Bantry   chantry   gantry   pantry

ANNUAL (*see* ANIEL)   ANY (*see* ENNY)

ANYARD

lanyard   Spaniard   tan-yard

106

ANZA

stanza   bonanza   extravaganza   Sancho Panza
     (*"Kansas" for plurals.*)

APAL (*see* APLE)   APEL (*see* APPLE)

APEN, APON

capon   misshapen   unshapen

APER, APIR, APOUR

caper   paper   tapir   vapour
     (*Extend* APE *for "draper," etc.*)

APHIC (*see* AFFIC)

APID

rapid   sapid   vapid

APIST

papist   (*And extend* APE *for "shapest," etc.*)

APLE, APAL

maple   papal   staple   Naples (*for plurals*)

APLESS

capless   chapless   hapless   sapless
strapless   tapless   wrapless

APLING, APPLING

grappling   knappling   sapling

APNEL

grapnel   shrapnel

APOUR (*see* APER)   APPER (*extend* AP)

APPET

lappet   tappet

APPLE, APEL

| apple | chapel | dapple | grapple |
| knapple | scapple | scrapple | thrapple |

APPY

chappie   happy   (*And extend* **AP.**)

APTER, APTOR

apter   captor   chapter   adaptor

APTION

caption   adaption   collapsion   contraption

APTIST, APTEST

aptest   Baptist   adaptest   Anabaptist

APTURE

capture   rapture   enrapture

ARAB

Arab   scarab

ARBER, ARBOR
arbor   barber   harbor

ARBERED, ARBOARD
barbered   harbored   larboard   starboard

ARBLE, ARBEL
barbel   garble   marble

ARCEL
marcel   parcel   tarsal   tarsel
(False rhymes in "castle," "Newcastle," etc.)

ARCHER
archer   marcher   starcher   departure

ARCHY
Archy   starchy   Karachi

ARDEN, ARDON
garden   harden   pardon   Hawarden

ARDER
ardour   larder   "Nevada"   *(Extend ARD.)*

ARDY
hardy   lardy   mardy   tardy
Coolgardie   foolhardy

AREA, ARIER
area   charier   hairier   warier
Bavaria   Berengaria   Bulgaria   wistaria

AREL, ARREL, AROL

barrel	carol	Carroll	Darrell
apparel	(*"Harold" for past tense.*)		

AREM, ARUM

Aram	harem	Sarum	alarum
harum-scarum			

ARET, ARAT, ARRET, ARROT

arret	Barratt	carat	caret
carrot	claret	garret	parrot

ARGENT

argent	sergeant

ARGO, ARGOT

argot	cargo	Dargo	largo
Margot	embargo	supercargo	(*Compare* AGO.)

ARIAN, ARYAN

aryan	abecedarian	agrarian	Bavarian
barbarian	Bulgarian	centenarian	cessarian
disciplinarian	grammarian	librarian	predestinarian
proletarian	Rotarian	valetudinarian	vulgarian

ARIAT, ARIOT

chariot	Harriet	lariat	Marriott
Marryatt	Iscariot		

ARIC

Garrick	barbaric	Pindaric

110

ARICE, ARRIS

Clarice   Harris   Paris

ARID, ARRIED

arid   carried   harried   married
parried   tarried   miscarried

ARING, AIRING, EARING

charing   hair-ring
(*Extend* ARE, AIR, EAR *for "caring," "airing," "swearing," etc.*)

ARION, ARRION

carrion   clarion   Marion   Hilarion

ARIOUS

Darius   Marius   various   bifarious
contrarious   gregarious   nefarious   ovarious
precarious   vicarious   multifarious   temerarious

ARISH, EARISH

bearish   fairish   garish   rarish
sparish   squarish

ARITY

charity   clarity   parity   rarity
angularity   dissimilarity   irregularity   jocularity
particularity   perpendicularity   popularity   regularity
secularity   similarity   singularity   vulgarity

ARKEN

darken   hearken

ARKER

Osaka   (*Extend* ARK *for "barker," etc.*)

111

ARKET

market   parquet   Newmarket

ARKLE

sparkle   hierarchal   matriarchal   monarchal
patriarchal

ARKLING

darkling   sparkling

ARKLY

darkly   sparkly   starkly

ARKY, AKI

barky	darkie	heark'ee	khaki
larky	marquee	parky	saki
sparky	Starkey	hierarchy	matriarchy
oligarchy	patriarchy		

ARLER, ARLOUR

marler   parlor   snarler   Transvaaler
     (*Compare* ALA.)

ARLET

scarlet   starlit   varlet

ARLEY, ARLY

barley   Charlie   gnarly   Marley
parley   snarly
     (*And extend* AR *for "particularly," etc.*)

ARLIC

garlic   Harlech

ARLING

darling	marling	snarling	sparling
starling			

ARLOW

Barlow	Carlow	Harlow	Marlow

ARLY (*see* ARLEY)

ARMER, ARMOUR

armor   Parma

(And extend ARM *for "charmer," etc.)*

ARMEST, ALARMIST

alarmist

(And extend ARM *for "harmest," etc. Compare* ALMIST.)

ARMY, ALMY

army	balmy	barmy	psalmy
smarmy			

ARNAL, ARNEL

carnal	charnel	darnel	Farnol

ARNER

darner	garner	yarner	(*Compare* ANA.)

ARNET, ARNESS

Barnet	garnet	incarnate	farness
harness			

ARNEY

barney	blarney	Carney	Killarney
ranee			

113

ARNISH

garnish   tarnish   varnish

ARPER

carper   harper   scarper   sharper

ARRACK

arrack   barrack   carrack

ARRANT

arrant   apparent   transparent

ARRANT (*broad*), ORRENT

torrent   warrant   abhorrent

ARRAS

arras   Arras   harass   embarrass

ARREL (*see* AREL)   ARREL (*broad, as in "quarrel," see* ORAL)

ARREN, ARON

Arran   baron   barren   fanfaron
McLaren

ARREN (*broad*)

warren   foreign   sporran

ARRIAGE, ARAGE

carriage   Harwich   marriage   disparage
inter-marriage   miscarriage

ARRIER

barrier	carrier	farrier	harrier
marrier	parrier	tarrier	

ARRIER (*broad*), ORRIOR

quarrier	sorrier	warrior

ARROW

arrow	barrow	Barrow	farrow
harrow	Harrow	Jarrow	marrow
narrow	sparrow	yarrow	Yarrow

ARRY

Barry	Carrie	carry	harry
Harry	Larry	marry	parry
tarry	miscarry	intermarry	

ARRY (*long*)

sparry	starry	tarry (*from "tar"*)

ARSHAL, ARTIAL

marshal	martial	partial	impartial

ARSLEY

parsley	sparsely

ARSON

arson	Carson	parson	squarson

ARTAN, ARTEN

Barton	carton	hearten	marten
smarten	Spartan	tartan	dishearten
kindergarten			

ARTAR, ARTER

barter	carter	charter	darter
garter	martyr	parter	Satyr
smarter	starter	tartar	tarter
imparter	self-starter		

ARTEL

cartel   startle

ARTFUL

artful   cartful   heartful

ARTIST, ARTEST

artist   chartist

(*Extend* ART *for "smartest," etc.*)

ARTLET

martlet	partlet	tartlet	Bartlett

ARTNER

partner	heartener	smartener	disheartener

ARTRIDGE

cartridge   cart-ridge   partridge

ARTY

arty	hearty	parti	party
smarty	Astarte	Clancarty	ecarté

ARVEL

carvel   Darvel   marvel

116

ARVEST

carvest   harvest   starvest

ARY (*see* AIRY)

ASAL, AZEL

hazel   nasal

ASCAL, ASCHAL   ASCAR (*see* ASKER)

paschal   rascal

ASCENT

nascent   renascent   (*And see* ACENT)

ASCOT

Ascot   mascot

ASEMENT

basement	casement	abasement	debasement
defacement	displacement	effacement	emplacement
interlacement	misplacement	replacement	

ASHEN, ASHION, ASSION, ATION (*short*)

ashen   fashion   passion   ration
compassion   dispassion

ASHER

rasher   haberdasher
(*And extend* ASH *for "masher," etc.*)

ASHY

ashy   flashy   mashie   sachet
splashy   trashy

ASIA

Asia	Dacia	fascia	acacia
Alsatia	Dalmatia	fantasia	

ASIN, ASON, ASTEN

basin	chasten	hasten	Jason
mason			

ASIS (*see* ACIS)

ASKER, ASCA, ASCAR

asker	basker	lascar	masker
tasker	Alaska	Madagascar	Nebraska

ASKET

basket	casket	gasket

ASPER

asper	clasper	gasper	grasper
jasper	Jasper	rasper	

ASSEL

castle	tassel	vassal

ASSES

molasses	(*And extend* ASS *for "asses," etc.*)

ASSET, ACET, ACIT

asset	basset	Brassett	facet
tacit			

ASSIC

classic	boracic	Jurassic	thoracic

ASSION (*see* ASHEN)

118

ASSIVE

massive   passive   impassive

ASSOCK

bassock   cassock   hassock

ASSY

brassie	brassy	chassis	classy
gassy	glacé	grassy	Jassy
lassie	massy	passé	Coomassie
Haile Selassie	Malagassy		

ASTARD, ASTERED

bastard	castored	dastard	mastered
plastered			

ASTEN (*see* ASIN)

ASTER (*short*)

aster	caster	castor	faster
master	pastor	plaster	vaster
alabaster	burgomaster	disaster	piastre
quartermaster			

ASTER (*long*)

baster	chaster	haster	paster
taster	waster	poetaster	

ASTIC

drastic	mastic	plastic	bombastic
ecclesiastic	elastic	enthusiastic	fantastic
gymnastic	Hudibrastic	iconoclastic	metaphrastic
monastic	periphrastic	pleonastic	sarcastic
scholastic			

ASTLY

ghastly   lastly   vastly

ASTY (*as in "pasty."*)

hasty   pasty   tasty

ASTY (*as in "nasty."*)

nasty   vasty

ATA (*as in "data."*)

data   strata   postulata   ultimata

ATA (*as in "cantata."*)

strata   cantata   errata   pro rata
sonata   (*Compare* ARTER.)

ATAL

datal   fatal   natal

ATAN (*see* AITEN)

ATANT, ATENT

blatant   latent   natant   **patent**

ATCHET

Datchet   hatchet   latchet   **ratchet**

ATCHMAN

Scotchman   watchman

ATCHY

batchy	patchy	scratchy

ATER, ATOR

cater	crater	freighter	gaiter
greater	Hayter	mater	pater
straighter	traitor	waiter	alligator
commentator	cunctator	curator	equator
gladiator	scrutator	spectator	testator
valuator			

(*Extend* ATE *for about* 200 *other good rhymes. Thus* "*hater*," "*navigator*," *etc.*)

ATHER (*short*)

blather	gather	lather	rather

ATHER (*long*)

farther	father

ATHING (*see* AYTHING)

ATHOS

Athos	bathos	pathos

ATIAL (*see* ACIAL)

ATIC

attic	static	acrobatic	Adriatic
aerostatic	aquatic	aromatic	Asiatic
asthmatic	chromatic	climatic	dematic
dogmatic	dramatic	ecstatic	emblematic
emphatic	epigrammatic	erratic	fanatic
grammatic	Hanseatic	hydrostatic	idiomatic

121

mathematic	morganatic	muriatic	pancreatic
phlegmatic	pneumatic	pragmatic	prismatic
quadratic	rheumatic	schismatic	spermatic
stigmatic	symptomatic	systematic	traumatic

ATIN

Latin	matin	patin	satin
Prestatyn			

ATION, ATIAN

nation	ration	station	abbreviation
abdication	aberration	abjuration	ablation
abnegation	abomination	abrogation	accentuation
accumulation	accusation	actualization	adaptation
adjudication	administration	admiration	adoration
adulation	adulteration	adumbration	advocation
aeration	affectation	affidation	affirmation
afflation	agitation	aggravation	aggregation
agglomeration	alcoholization	alienation	alimentation
allegation	alleviation	alliteration	allocation
Alsatian	alteration	altercation	alternation
amalgamation	ambulation	amplification	amputation
anatomization	anhelation	animation	annexation
annihilation	annotation	annunciation	anticipation
appellation	application	approbation	appropriation
approximation	arbitration	argumentation	aromatization
arrogation	articulation	aspiration	assassination
assentation	asseveration	assignation	assimilation
association	attenuation	attestation	augmentation
auguration	auscultation	authorization	aviation
avocation	bifurcation	cachination	calcination
calculation	calumniation	cancellation	canonization
capitation	capitulation	captivation	carbonization
carnation	carnification	cassation	castigation
castration	causation	celebration	cementation
citation	civilization	clarification	classification
coagulation	cogitation	cognomination	cohabitation
collation	collimation	collocation	colonization
coloration	combination	commemoration	commendation
compensation	compilation	complication	compurgation
computation	concentration	conciliation	condemnation
condensation	condonation	confabulation	confederation

122

configuration	confirmation	confiscation	conflagration
conformation	confrontation	confutation	congelation
congratulation	congregation	conjugation	connotation
conservation	consideration	consolation	consolidation
contamination	contemplation	continuation	conversation
convocation	co-operation	co-ordination	copulation
coronation	correlation	corroboration	corrugation
coruscation	creation	cremation	crepitation
culmination	cultivation	cumulation	cunctation
curtation	curvation	dalmatian	damnation
debilitation	decimation	declamation	declaration
declination	decoration	decrustation	decussation
dedication	defalcation	defamation	defecation
defloration	degeneration	degradation	degustation
deification	delectation	delegation	delineation
dementation	demobilization	demonstration	denomination
denudation	denunciation	deodorization	depopulation
deportation	depreciation	depredation	deprivation
deputation	derivation	derogation	desecration
desiccation	designation	desolation	despoliation
destination	detestation	deterioration	determination
detonation	detruncation	devastation	deviation
dictation	differentiation	digitation	dignification
dilapidation	dilation	disapprobation	disclamation
disinclination	disintegration	dislocation	disobligation
disorganization	dispensation	disputation	dissemination
dissertation	dissimilation	dissipation	distillation
divagation	divarication	divination	domination
dotation	dubation	dulcification	duration
ebonification	economization	edentation	edification
education	edulcoration	effemination	ejaculation
elaboration	elation	electrification	elevation
elicitation	elimination	elongation	elutriation
emanation	emancipation	emasculation	embarkation
embrocation	emendation	emulation	enervation
enumeration	epuration	equalization	equation
equitation	equivocation	estimation	estivation
etiolation	evacuation	evagation	evagination
evangelization	evaporation	evocation	exacerbation
exaggeration	exaltation	examination	exasperation
excruciation	execration	exemplification	exhalation
exhilaration	exhortation	exhumation	exoneration

expiation	expiration	expiscation	explanation
explication	exploitation	exploration	exportation
expostulation	expurgation	extenuation	extermination
extirpation	extrication	exudation	exultation
exundation	fabrication	falcation	fascination
felicitation	fenestration	fermentation	ferrumination
fertilization	festination	figuration	filtration
fixation	flagellation	flagration	flammation
flirtation	florification	fluctuation	foliation
fomentation	formation	formication	fornication
fortification	fossilization	foundation	fructification
frumentation	frustration	fulmination	fumigation
furfuration	gelatination	gemnation	generalization
generation	germination	gestation	gesticulation
glaciation	glomeration	glorification	gravitation
gubernation	gustation	gyration	habitation
hallucination	hesitation	hibernation	hortation
humanization	humiliation	hypothecation	identification
illegitimization	illimitation	illiteration	illumination
illustration	imagination	immaculation	immanation
impersonation	imperturbation	implication	importation
imprecation	impregnation	impropriation	improvisation
imputation	inaffectation	inanimation	inapplication
inarticulation	inauguration	incantation	incapacitation
incarceration	incarnation	inceration	incineration
incitation	inclination	inconsideration	incorporation
incrimination	incrustation	incubation	inculcation
indication	indignation	indiscrimination	induration
inebriation	infatuation	infestation	infeudation
inflammation	inflation	information	ingemination
initiation	innervation	innovation	inoculation
inosculation	insanitation	insinuation	insolation
interpretation	interrogation	intimation	intonation
intoxication	inundation	investigation	invitation
invocation	irradiation	irrigation	irritation
isolation	iteration	jacitation	jaculation
jobation	jollification	jubilation	judaization
justification	laceration	lachrymation	lactation
lamentation	lapidation	lapidification	lauration
lavation	legation	legislation	legitimation
levigation	levitation	libation	libration
licentiation	ligation	limitation	lineation

liquation	liquidation	location	lubrication
lucubration	luctation	ludification	lunation
lustration	maceration	machination	mactation
manducation	manifestation	masticulation	matriculation
mediation	medication	meditation	melioration
mellification	mensuration	migration	ministration
moderation	modification	modulation	molestation
mollification	moralization	mordication	mortification
multiplication	mutation	mutilation	mystification
narration	natation	nationalization	naturalization
nauseation	navigation	negation	negotiation
nictitation	nidification	nidulation	noctambulation
nodation	nomination	notation	notification
novation	nudation	nugation	nullification
numeration	nutation	obduration	obtestation
occulation	occupation	operation	oration
orbiculation	organization	origination	oscillation
oscultation	ossification	oxidation	oxygenation
pabulation	pacification	pagination	palliation
palpation	palpitation	panification	participation
pauperization	peculation	penetration	perambulation
percolation	perduration	peregrination	perforation
permeation	permutation	pernoctation	peroration
perscrutation	personation	personification	perspiration
perturbation	petrification	polarization	polliation
postillation	postulation	precipitation	predestination
predication	prefiguration	prejudication	prelation
premeditation	preoccupation	preparation	preponderation
preservation	prestidigitation	prevarication	prerelation
privation	probation	proclamation	procrastination
procreation	procuration	profanation	prognostication
prolation	prolification	prolongation	promulgation
pronunciation	propagation	propitiation	prorogation
provocation	publication	pulsation	punctuation
qualification	quotation	racemation	radiation
ramification	ratification	ratiocination	realization
recalcitration	recantation	recapitulation	reciprocation
recitation	reclamation	reclimination	recolonization
recreation	recrimination	rectification	recubation
redintegration	reduplication	re-examination	reformation
refrigeration	refutation	regeneration	registration
regulation	regurgitation	re-importation	reintegration

reiteration	rejuvenation	relation	relaxation
relegation	remonstration	remuneration	renovation
renunciation	reorganization	reparation	replication
representation	reprobation	repudiation	reservation
resignation	respiration	restoration	resuscitation
retaliation	retardation	retractation	revelation
revivication	revocation	regation	reogation
rotation	ructation	rumination	salivation
salutation	salvation	sanctification	sanguification
satiation	saturation	scintillation	secularization
sensation	separation	sequestration	serration
siccation	signation	signification	simulation
situation	solicitation	solidification	sophistication
specialization	specification	speculation	spiritualization
spoliation	stabilization	stagnation	stellation
sternutation	stimulation	stipulation	stratification
stridulation	stultification	stylobation	subjugation
sublevation	subligation	sublimation	sublineation
subluxation	subordination	subornation	subrogation
succusation	sudation	suffocation	sulphuration
suppuration	suspiration	sustenation	syllabification
tartarization	taxation	temporization	temptation
tentation	tergiversation	termination	testamentation
testation	testification	thurification	titillation
titurbation	toleration	tralation	tranquillization
transformation	translation	transmigration	transmutation
triangulation	tribulation	triplication	trepidation
truncation	turbination	ulceration	ululation
undervaluation	undulation	usurpation	vacation
vacillation	validation	valuation	vaporization
variegation	vaticination	vegetation	venation
venenation	veneration	ventilation	verbilization
vermiculation	vernation	versification	vesication
vexation	vibration	vigesimation	vilification
vindication	violation	visitation	vitiation
vitriolation	vituperation	vivification	vocalization
vocation	vociferation	volatilization	volcanization
vulcanization	vulneration		

ATIST (*see* ATTEST)

ATIVE, ATIFF

caitiff	dative	native	aggregative
creative	educative	operative	predicative
procreative	provocative		

ATLING, ATTLING

| battling | fatling | gatling | prattling |
| rattling | spratling | tattling | tittle-tattling |

ATO

| Cato | Plato | potato |

ATOR (*see* ATER)

ATRAP

| bat-trap | cat-trap | rat-trap | satrap |

ATRIX

| hat-tricks | matrix | administratrix | mediatrix |
| testatrix | | | |

ATRON

| matron | patron |

ATTEN, ATON, ATEN

| baton | batten | fatten | flatten |
| paten | patten | ratten | |

ATTER

batter	blatter	chatter	clatter
fatter	flatter	hatter	latter
matter	patter	platter	scatter
shatter	smatter	spatter	tatter
bespatter			

ATTERN, ATURN

| pattern | Saturn | slattern |

ATTEST, ATIST, ATTICED

| bratticed | fattest | latticed | statist |

(And extend AT for "flattest," etc.)

ATTLE

| battle | cattle | prattle | rattle |
| tattle | Seattle | tittle-tattle | |

ATTLER, ATLER

| tatler | *(And extend ATTLE.)* |

ATTO, ATTEAU

| chateau | gateau | plateau | mulatto |

ATTY

batty	catty	chatty	fatty
gnatty	natty	Patti	patty
ratty	scatty	Cincinnati	

ATUM

| datum | stratum | eratum | pomatum |
| postulatum | ultimatum | | |

ATURE (*long*)

| nature | legislature | nomenclature |

ATURE (*short*), ATCHER

stature

(There is no good rhyme to this, but extensions of ACH and ATCH may be permitted, as in "catcher," "attacher," etc.)

ATUS

| status | afflatus | apparatus | hiatus |

ATY, EIGHTY, ATEY

| eighty | Haiti | Katie | matey |
| slaty | weighty | | |

AUCER

| Chaucer | saucer | (*Compare* OARSER.) |

AUCUS

| caucus | Dorcas | raucous |

AUCTION

| auction | concoction | decoction |

AUDAL

| caudal | caudle | dawdle |

AUDIT

| audit | plaudit |

AUDY, AWDY

| bawdy | gaudy | Geordie | lordy |
| Maudie | | | |

AUFFEUR

| chauffeur | gopher | loafer | sofa |

AUGHTER (*as in* "*laughter,*" *see* AFTER)

AUGHTER (*as in "daughter"*)

daughter   slaughter   tauter   manslaughter
     (*Compare* ORTER.)

AUGHTY

haughty   naughty   (*Compare* ORTY.)

AULIC

aulic   hydraulic   (*Compare* OLIC.)

AULTER (*see* ALTAR)

AULTY

faulty   malty   salty   vaulty

AUNDER

launder   maunder

AUNTER

chaunter   gaunter   haunter   saunter
taunter   vaunter

AUPER

pauper   torpor   warper

AUSEOUS, AUTIOUS

cautious   nauseous

AUSER, AWSER

causer   hawser   pauser   Mauser

AUSTRAL

austral   claustral

AUTION

caution   precaution   (*Compare* ORTION.)

AVA

Ava   guava   Java   lava
larva   palaver

(*Compare "carver" and other extensions of* ARVE.)

AVAGE

lavage   ravage   savage

AVAL, AVEL

naval   navel   save-all   **Wavell**

AVEL (*short*)

cavil   gavel   gravel   **ravel**
Savile   travel   unravel

AVELIN

javelin   ravelin

AVEMENT

pavement   enslavement

AVEN

craven   graven   haven   raven
shaven   engraven   New Haven

AVER (*see* AVOUR)

AVERN, AVID

cavern	tavern	avid	gravid

AVIOUR

pavior	saviour	wavier	Batavia
behavior	Belgravia	Moravia	

AVIS

avis	Davis	mavis	Mavis

AVISH (*short*)

lavish	ravish	McTavish

AVISH (*long*)

knavish	slavish

AVOUR, AVER

favor	flavor	savor	disfavor
semi-quaver	(*Extend* AVE *for* "braver," *etc.*)		

AVY

cavy	Davy	gravy	navy
slavey	wavy	peccavi!	

AVVY

navvy	savvy

AWDRY

Audrey	bawdry	tawdry

AWDY (*see* AUDY)   AWKER (*see* ALKER)

132

AWFUL

awful   lawful

AWKY, ALKY

gawky   pawky   *"talkie"*   Milwaukee
    (*Extend* ALK *for "stalky," etc. Compare* ORKY.)

AWNING

awning
    (*Extend* AWN *and* ORN *for "dawning," "morning," etc.*)

AWNY

brawny   fawny   Pawnee   sawney
scrawny   Shawnee   tawny   yawny
mulligatawny (*Compare* ORNY.)

AWYER

lawyer   sawyer

AXEN, AXON

flaxen   Jackson   Saxon   waxen

AXY

flaxy   Laxey   taxi   waxy
ataxy

AYDAY, EYDAY

heyday   payday   playday   May Day

AYER, EYOR
(*Extend* AY *and* EY *for "gayer," "surveyor," etc.*)

AYMAN

cayman	Damon	drayman	flamen
hay-man	layman	Ramon	highwayman

AYTHING

bathing	plaything	scathing	swathing

AZA

Gaza	plaza	Zaza

AZARD

brassard	hazard	mazard

AZEL (*see* ASAL)

AZEN, AZON, AISIN

blazon	brazen	raisin	diapason
emblazon			

AZOR, AISER

praiser	Fraser	razor

(*And extend* AISE *and* AZE.)

AZIER

brazier	crazier	glazier	hazier
lazier			

AZY, AISY

crazy	daisy	Daisy	hazy
lazy	mazy	Maisie	quasi

AZZLE

| Basil | dazzle | drazil | frazzle |
| razzle | bedazzle | razzle-dazzle | |

EA

| idea | Korea | Judea | panacea |
| ratifia | | | |

EACHER, EATURE, EECHER

creature   feature   (*And extend* EACH *and* EECH)

EACHY (*extend* EACH)

EACON

| beacon | deacon | weaken |

EADEN (*short*)

| deaden | Heddon | leaden | redden |
| Sedden | threaden | | |

EADER, EDAR, EDER, EEDER

cedar   (*And extend* EAD, EDE *and* EED.)

EADLE, EEDLE

| beadle | Cheadle | daedal | needle |
| predal | tweedle | wheedle | bipedal |

EADLOCK

| deadlock | wedlock |

EADWAY

| dead-way | headway | Medway |

EADY (*short, see* EDDY)   EADY (*long, see* EEDY)

EAFER

deafer   heifer   zephyr   Strathpeffer
"*whateffer*"

EAFEST

deafest   prefaced

EAFY, EEFY

beefy   feoffee   Fifi   leafy
reefy   sheafy

EAGER, EAGRE, EAGUER, IGUER

eager   leaguer   meagre   beleaguer
intriguer

EAGLE, EGAL

beagle   eagle   gregal   legal
regal   sea-gull   illegal   inveigle

EAKEN (*see* EACON)

EAKER, EEKER

beaker   speaker   (*And extend* EAK, EEK.)

EAKING

sea-king
      (*And extend* EAK *and* EEK *for* "speaking," "seeking," *etc.*)

EAKLING

meekling   treacling   weakling

EAKY, EEKY

beaky   cheeky   cliquey
      (*And extend* EAK.)

136

EAL

real   ideal   unreal   hymeneai

(Compare EAL and EEL in one-syllable rhymes.)

EALER, EELER, EALING *(extend EAL and EEL in one-syllable rhymes.)*

EALOT *(see ELATE)*

EALOUS

jealous   zealous   Marcellus

EALTHY

healthy   stealthy   wealthy

EALTY

fealty   realty

EALY

Ely	freely	Healy	mealy
squealy	steely	genteely	Matabele
ukulele			

EAMAN, EEMAN, EMAN, EMON

beeman	demon	freeman	gleeman
he-man	leman	seaman	semen
tea-man			

EAMER, EMER, EMUR

Braemar   emir   femur   lemur

(And extend words under EAM for "dreamer," "schemer," etc.)

EAMISH

beamish   dreamish   squeamish

EAMSTER *(see EEMSTER)*

EAMY

| creamy | dreamy | seamy | streamy |

EAN, IEN, IAN

Ian	lien	pæan	Korean
empyrean	epicurean	European	Fijian
Hawaiian	herculean	hymenean	Jacobean
Judean	plebian	pygmean	Pythagorean

EANER, EANOUR

demeanour

> (*And extend words under* EAN *for* "greener," "cleaner,"
> "obscener," *etc.*)

EANEST, EENIST, ENIST

plenist   machinist

> (*Extend words under* EAN *in one-syllable rhymes for*
> "cleanest," "obscenist," *etc.*)

EANING, EANLY, EENLY, ENELY, EAPER, EEPER, EEPY (*see one-syllable rhymes and extend*)

EANO

| beano | Reno | Albino | bambino |
| casino | maraschino | merino | Filipino |

EARANCE, ERENCE, EARER, EARCHER, IRCHER, URCHER (*see* EAR, EARCH, IRCH, *etc., and extend.*)

EAREST, ERIST

merest   querist   theorist

> (*And extend* EAR, EER *and* ERE.)

EARETH, ERITH

Erith   (*Extend* EAR *for* "heareth," *etc.*)

138

EARFUL
cheerful   earful   fearful   tearful

EARIER, EERIER, ERIOR
eerier   anterior   inferior   interior
Liberia   posterior   Siberia   superior
(And extend EARY, EERY *for "wearier," "beerier," etc.)*

EARING, EERING
earring
(And extend EAR, EER *for "hearing," "leering," etc.)*

EARLY, IRLY, URLY
burly   curly   early   girlie
pearly   Purley   Shirley   twirly

EARLY, EERLY, ERELY
(Extend EAR, EER, ERE *for "clearly," "merely," etc.)*

EARMENT
cerement   endearment

EARNER, IRNER, URNER, EARNING, IRNING, URNING *(extend words under* EARN)

EARNESS, EERNESS
sheerness
(And extend EAR *and* EER *for "clearness," "queerness," etc.)*

EARNEST, ERNEST, URNEST
earnest   Ernest   furnaced
(And extend words under EARN *for "sternest," "burnest," etc.)*

EARY, EERY, ERY

Erie	eerie	dearie	Leary
peri	query	Dundreary	theory

(And extend EAR *and* EER *for "weary," "beery," etc.)*

EASAND

reasoned	seasoned	treasoned	weasand

EASANT, ESCENT

crescent	peasant	pheasant	pleasant
present	convalescent	decrescent	deliquescent
delitescent	effervescent	efflorescent	excrescent
incessant	obsolescent	phosphorescent	putrescent
quiescent			

EASAR, EASER

Cæsar	geezer	geyser	sizar
Ebenezer			

(And extend certain words under EASE.*)*

EASEL

Diesel	easel	measle	weasel

EASON

reason	season	treason

EASTER

Easter	northeaster	*(And extend* EAST.*)*

EASTING

bee-sting	feasting

EASTLY

beastly   priestly

EASURE, EISURE

leisure   measure   pleasure   treasure
displeasure

EASY, EEZY

breezy   cheesy   easy   freezy
greasy   queasy   sleazy   sneezy
wheezy   Brindisi

EATEN, EETEN

Beeton   Cretan   Eton   seton
(*And extend* EAT *and* EET *for "beaten," "sweeten," etc.*)

EATER, EETER, ETA, ETER, ETRE

beta   Greta   litre   meter
Peter   prætor   goldbeater   saltpeter
two-seater
(*Extend* EAT *and* EET.)

EATHER (*short*), ETHER

blether   feather   heather   Heather
leather   nether   tether   weather
wether   whether   altogether   together

EATHER (*long*)

breather   either   neither   seether

EATHING, EETHING

breathing   seething   tea-thing   teething
wreathing   bequeathing

EATURE

creature	feature	(*Compare* EACHER.)

EATY, EETY

Beattie	meaty	peaty	sleety
sweetie	Otaheiti	Tahiti	

EAVEN, EVEN

Bevan	Devon	Evan	Heaven
leaven	Leven	seven	eleven

EAVER

beaver	Belvoir	Eva	fever
leaver	lever	stiver	viva
Geneva	Siva		

(*And extend rhymes under* EAVE; *thus* "cleaver," "deceiver," *etc.*)

EAVY, EVY

bevy	chevvy	heavy	levy
levée	*"nevvy"*		

EBE

Bebe	Hebe	Phœbe

EBEL, EBBLE

pebble	rebel	treble

EEBLE

feeble	Keble

ECCA

Mecca	Rebecca	(*Compare* ECKER.)

ECENT

decent	puissant	recent	indecent

ECHER, ETCHER

etcher	fetcher	fletcher	lecher
retcher	sketcher	stretcher	

ECHO

echo	gecko	secco	"dekko"

ECIAN, ETION

Grecian	accretion	completion	depletion
deletion	excretion	Phœnician	repletion
secretion	Venetian		

ECIES

Decies	nieces	species	thesis

(Add "s" to certain words under EACE; *thus "fleeces,"*
"ceases," "mantelpieces," etc.)

ECIOUS

specious	facetious

ECKER, EQUER

"brekker"	Flecker	exchequer

(And extend ECK *and* EQUE. *Compare* ECCA.)

ECKLE, EKEL

freckle	heckle	keckle	shekel
speckle	*("Beccles" and "Eccles" for plurals.)*		

ECKLESS, ECKLACE

feckless	checkless	necklace	reckless
speckless			

143

ECKON

beckon   reckon

    (*Preterites of same to rhyme with "second" and "fecund."*)

ECTIC

hectic   eclectic   electric

ECTION, EXION *and* ECTIVE

flection   vection   complexion   invective

    (*And extend* ECT *and* EX *for* "section," "connection," "detective," "subjective," *etc.*)

ECTOR, ECTRE

hector	Hector	nectar	rector
specter	vector	(*And extend* ECT.)	

ECTURE

lecture   architecture   conjecture   prefecture

EDAL, EDDLE, EDULE

medal	meddle	pedal	peddle
reddle	schedule	treadle	intermeddle

EDAR

cedar   (*And extend* EAD *for* "pleader," *etc.*)

EDDY, EADY

eddy	Freddy	heady	Neddy
ready	shreddy	steady	Teddy
already			

EDEN

Eden   Sweden

EDENCE

credence   antecedence   precedence

EDENT

credent   needn't   sedent   antecedent

EDGER

edger   dredger   hedger   ledger
pledger   sledger   wedger

EDGWARE

Edgware   sledge-wear

EDIT

edit   credit   discredit   sub-edit

EDIUM

medium   tedium

EDLAR

medlar   meddler   pedlar   peddler
scheduler

EEDLESS, EEDLY (*extend* EAD *and* EED)

EDLEY, EADLY

deadly   medley   redly   Sedley

145

EDO

credo   Toledo   torpedo   lido
libido

EECHY, EACHY (*extend* EACH, EECH)

EECY

fleecy   greasy

EEDLESS, EEDY, EADY (*extend* EAD *and* EED)

EEMSTER

deemster   teamster

EENISH, EANISH (*extend* EAN *and* EEN *in one-syllable rhymes.*)

EENY, ENE

greeny   "tweenie"   Athene   nota-bene
Proserpine   Queenie

EEPIER

creepier   sleepier   leap-year

EEPLE, EOPLE

people   steeple

EERAGE

beerage   clearage   peerage   steerage

EESTONE

freestone   keystone   sea-stone

146

EETLE

beetle   betel   decretal

EEVISH, IEVISH

peevish   thievish

EEZER (*see* EASAR)

EFTY

hefty   lefty   wefty

EGAL (*see* EAGLE)

EGGAR, EGGER

beggar   dregger   egger   kegger
pegger

EGGY

dreggy   eggy   leggy   Meggie
Peggy

EGIAN, EGION

Fijian   legion   region   collegian
Glaswegian   Norwegian

EGNANT

pregnant   regnant

EGRESS

egress   negress   regress

EGRET

egret   regret

EIFER (*see* EAFER)

EIGHBOR *and* EIGHTY (*see* ABOR *and* ATY)

147

EIRESS

heiress   mayoress

EIST

deist	beest	fleest	freest
seest			

EITHER *("e" sounded)*

ether   (*And see* EATHER.)

EITHER *("i" sounded)*

blither	either	lither	mither
neither	scyther	tither	writher

ELATE, ELOT

helot	prelate	stellate	zealot
appellate	constellate		

ELDAM, ELDOM

beldam   seldom

ELDER, ELDEST, ELDING (*extend* ELD)

ELFISH

elfish   selfish   shell-fish

ELIC

relic   telic   angelic

ELINE

bee-line   feline   sea-line

148

ELISH, ELLISH

hellish   relish   embellish

ELLA

Bella   Ella   Stella   Arabella
prunella   umbrella   (*Compare* Eller.)

ELLER (*extend* ELL)

ELLIST, ELLISED

trellised   'cellist (*And extend* ELL *for* "*dwellest,*" *etc.*)

ELLO, ELLOE, ELLOW

bellow   'cello   fellow   mellow
yellow   duello   Martello   Portobello
prunello   Punchinello   violoncello

ELLY

belly   jelly   Kelly   Nelly
Shelley   smelly

ELON

felon   melon

ELPER

Belper   helper   yelper

ELSIE

Elsie   Chelsea   Selsey

ELTA, ELTER

delta   helter   shelter   skelter
smelter   svelter   swelter   welter
     (*And extend* ELT.)

EMBER

ember   member   December   dismember
November   remember   September

EMBLE

Kemble   tremble   assemble   dissemble
resemble

EMBLY

trembly   Wembley   assembly

EMI, EMMY

clemmy   demi   hemi   Jemmy
semi

EMIER, EAMIER

creamier   dreamier   premier   steamier

EMISES

nemesis   premises

EMISH

blemish   Flemish   phlegmish

EMIST

chemist   hemmest   premised   stemmest

EMLIN

Kremlin   gremlin   Fremlin

EMOR

hemmer   tremor   condemner

EMPLAR

templar   exemplar

EMPTION

emption   ademption   co-emption
pre-emption   redemption

EMU
emu   seamew

EMUR (*see* EAMER)

EMUSE
bemuse   emus   seamews

ENA

Ena	Lena	Nina	scena
Tina	Zena	arena	concertina
hyena	Iena	Modena	ocarina
patina	Pasadena	semolina	signorina
Tsarina			

(*And compare* EANER *and* EANOUR.)

ENACE, ENNIS, ENNOUS

Dennis	menace	pennous	tenace
tennis	Venice	impennous	vaginopennous

ENAL
penal   renal   venal   duodenal

ENANT
pennant   tenant   lieutenant

ENATE (*see* ENNET)

ENSA, ENCER
censer   censor   spencer
(*And extend* ENCE *and* ENSE *for "fencer," "denser," etc.*)

ENCEFORTH
henceforth   thenceforth

ENCHER, ENSURE, ENTURE

censure	venture	adventure	debenture
indenture	misadventure	peradventure	

(*And extend* ENCH *for "bencher," "quencher," etc.*)

151

ENCIL, ENSAL

mensal   pencil   stencil   prehensile
utensil

ENDANT, ENDENT

pendant   pendent   splendent   attendant
resplendent
     (*And extend* END *for "defendant," etc.*)

ENDER, ENDOR, ENDA

Brenda   fender   gender   slender
splendor   Zenda   surrender
     (*And extend* END *for "lender," "defender," etc.*)

ENDON

Hendon   tendon

ENGLISH

English   jinglish   tinglisb

ENGTHEN

lengthen   strengthen

ENIAL

genial   menial   venial   congenial

ENIC

scenic   splenic   arsenic (*adj.*)   eugenic
photogenic   (*Pluralize "scenic" to rhyme with "Phoenix."*)

ENIN

Benin   Lenin   Menin

ENIOR

senior   señor   signor   teenier
weenier

ENISH

rhenish   tenish   replenish

ENIST (*see* EANEST)

ENNA

henna   senna   duenna   Gehenna
sienna   Vienna

ENNEL

fennel   kennel   phenyl

ENNER, ENOR, ENOUR

tenor   tenour   (*And extend* EN.)

ENITH, ENNETH

Kenneth   zenith

ENNET, ENATE

Bennett   jennet   kennet   rennet
senate   tenet

ENNIS (*see* ENACE)

ENNON, ENON

pennon   tenon

ENNY, ANY

any   Benny   Denny   fenny
Jenny   many   penny   wenny
Abergavenny Kilkenny

ENSER (*see* ENCER)   ENSILE (*see* ENCIL)

ENSIVE
pensive   (*And extend* ENCE *and* ENSE *for* "expensive," *etc.*)

ENSION (*see* ENTIAN)

ENTAIL
entail   ventail

ENTAL, ENTIL, ENTLE
dental   gentle   lentil   mental
rental   trental
    (*And extend* ENT *for* "accidental," "ornamental," *etc.*)

ENTANCE, ENTENCE
sentence   repentance

ENTER, ENTOR
centaur   center   enter   mentor
    (*And extend* ENT *for* "renter," "tormentor," *etc.*)

ENTIAN, ENTION, ENSIAN
gentian   mention   pension   tension
abstention accension   ascension   convention
detention   dimension   dissension   intension
intention   intervention   supervention
    (*And extend* END *and* ENT *for* "distension," "attention,"
        etc.)

ENTICE, ENTIS
pentice   prentice   apprentice   compos mentis

ENTILE
Gentile   pentile

ENTIST, ENTEST, ENTICED
dentist   prenticed   apprenticed
   (*And extend* ENT *for "scentest," etc.*)

ENTLE, ENTIL (*see* ENTAL)

ENTRAL
central   ventral

ENTRY
entry	gentry	sentry	comment'ry
element'ry	invent'ry	parliament'ry	

ENTURE
denture	venture	adventure	debenture
indenture	misadventure	peradventure	

   (*And compare* ENCHER.)

ENTY
plenty	scenty	twenty	dolce far niente
festina lente			

ENU
menu   venue

ENUS
genus   Venus

EO
Cleo	Leo	Rio	trio
yeo			

EOLE
creole   key-hole

EON
æon	Ian	Leon	neon
peon	Fijian	Hawaiian	plebeian

155

EOPARD, EPHERD, EPPERED
leopard peppered shepherd

EPID
tepid trepid intrepid

EPOT
Beppo depot Aleppo

EPPER, EPER
leper pepper stepper

EPPING
Epping stepping

EPPY
peppy Sheppey

EPTIC
peptic sceptic septic antiseptic
dyspeptic enpeptic epileptic

EPTOR
sceptre acceptor preceptor interceptor

EQUAL, EQUEL
equal sequel co-equal unequal

EQUENCE
frequence sequence

ERA
era lira Vera chimera

(*Compare* EARER, *for which extend* EAR.)

ERALD

Gerald	ferruled	herald	imperilled

ERBAL, URBLE

burble	herbal	verbal

ERCER, ERSER, URSAR

bursar	curser	mercer	nurser
purser	(*And extend* ERSE *for "terser," etc.*)		

ERCY, URSY

Circe	mercy	nursey	Percy
pursy	controversy	grammercy	

EREAL, ERIAL

cereal	ferial	serial	arterial
ethereal	funereal	immaterial	imperial
material	ministerial	venereal	

ERGER, ERDURE, URGER

burgher	merger	perjure	purger
scourger	urger	verdure	verger
deterger			

ERET (*see* ERIT)

ERGY, IRGY, URGY

clergy	dirgy	sergy	surgy

ERIC, ERRICK

Berwick	cleric	Derek	derrick
Eric	ferric	Herrick	Lerwick

| spheric | atmospheric | enteric | generic |
| hemispheric | Homeric | hysteric | numeric |

ERIL, ERRULE, ERYL
| beryl | Beryl | Errol | ferrule |
| Merrall | peril | spherule | |

ERISH
cherish   perish

ERIT, ERRET
| ferret | merit | demerit | disinherit |
| inherit | | | |

ERJURE (*see* ERGER)

ERKIN
| firkin | gherkin | jerkin | merkin |
| Perkin | | | |

ERKY, URKY
| jerky | murky | perky | smirky |
| turkey | Turkey | | |

ERLING (*see* IRLING)

ERMAN, ERMON
| Burman | Firman | German | Herman |
| merman | sermon | Omdurman | |

ERMENT
| ferment | averment | bestirment | determent |
| interment | preferment | | |

ERMIN, ERMINE
| ermine | vermin | determine | predetermine |

ERMIT

hermit   Kermit   permit (*noun*)   "termit"

ERNAL, ERNEL, OLONEL, OURNAL, URNAL

colonel	journal	kernel	sternal
vernal	diurnal	eternal	external
hodiernal	infernal	internal	fraternal
maternal	nocturnal	paternal	sempiternal
supernal			

ERNARD

Bernard   gurnard

ERO

hero	Nero	pierrot	zero
bandolero	bolero	montero	sombrero

ERRAND

errand   gerund

ERRIER

burier   ferrier   merrier   terrier

ERING

derring   herring

ERY (*as in "query," see* EARY)   ERRULE (*see* ERIL)

ERRY

berry	bury	Bury	cherry
Derry	ferry	jerry	Kerry
merry	perry	sherry	skerry
very	wherry	Londonderry	Pondicherry

ERSEY, URZY

furzy	jersey	Jersey	kersey
Mersey	New Jersey		

ERSIAN, ERSION, ERTIAN, URSION

mersion	Persian	tertian	version
abstention	animadversion	aspersion	assertion
aversion	coercion	conversion	demersion
desertion	detersion	dispersion	diversion
emersion	excursion	exertion	immersion
incursion	insertion	inversion	perversion
reversion	subversion		

ERSON, ORSEN

person	urson	worsen	McPherson

ERSUS

thyrsus	versus

ERTAIN, URTAIN

Burton	certain	curtain	Girton
Merton	uncertain		

ERTER, IRTER, URTER, ERTEST, ERTLY, URTLY
(*extend* ERT, IRT *and* URT)

ERVANT, ERVENT

fervent	servant	observant

ERVER, ERVOR
fervor	(*And extend* ERVE *for* "server," *etc.*)

ERVID

fervid	scurvied	perfervid

(*And accentuate final syllables of certain words in* ERVE
and URVE. *Thus* "curved," *etc.*)

ERVISH

curvish	dervish	nervish	swervish

ERVY, URVY

curvy	nervy	scurvy	topsy-turvy

ESAGE, ESSAGE

message   presage

ESCENCE, ESSENCE

essence	adolescence	coalescence	convalescence
delitescence	effervescence	efflorescence	excrescence
obsolescence	phosphorescence	pubescence	putrescence
quiescence	quintessence	senescence	turgescence

ESCIENCE

nescience   prescience

ESCO

fresco   Tresco   alfresco

ESCU

fescue   rescue

ESENCE, EASANCE

pleasance   presence   omnipresence

ESION

lesion	adhesion	cohesion	Ephesian
inhesion	magnesion	Polynesian	

ESIS

species   thesis   aposiopesis   exegesis

(*And extend certain words under* EACE *for "ceases," etc.*)

ESSAGE (*see* ESAGE)

ESSENCE (*see* ESCENCE)   ESSEL (*see* ESTLE)

ESSER, ESSOR

dresser   lesser   lessor   messer
presser   (*And extend* ESS *for "transgressor," etc.*)

ESION

session   concession   discretion   secession
(*And extend* ESS *for "profession," etc.*)

ESSURE

pressure   (*And extend* ESH *for "flesher," "refresher," etc.*)

ESSY

Bessie   Crecy   dressy   essay
Jessie   messy   Tessie

ESTAL, ESTLE

festal   pestle   vestal

ESTER

Chester   Esther   fester   Hester
jester   Leicester   sou'wester
(*And extend* EST *for "tester," "molester," etc.*)

ESTIAL

bestial   celestial

ESTIGE

prestige   vestige

ESTINE

destine   mess-tin   clandestine   intestine
predestine

ESTIVE

estive	festive	restive	digestive
investive	suggestive		

ESTLE (*silent "t"*)

Cecil	nestle	trestle	vessel
wrestle	(*Extend above for rhymes to* ESTLER.)		

ESTO

presto   manifesto

ESTRAL, ESTREL

kestrel   ancestral   orchestral

ESTURE

gesture   vesture   divesture

ESTY

chesty	resty	testy	yesty

ETCHER (*see* ECHER)

ETHEL

Bethel   Ethel   methyl

ETFUL (*extend* ET *for "fretful," "forgetful," etc.*)

ETHER (*see* EATHER)　　ETOR, ETER
(*see* EATER)

ETTER, ETTOR

fetter　　(*And extend* ET *for "better," "debtor," etc.*)

ETTISH, ETISH

fetish　　Lettish　　(*And extend* ET *for "pettish," etc.*)

ETTLE, ETAL

fettle	kettle	metal	mettle
nettle	petal	settle	unsettle

ETTO

ghetto	petto	falsetto	lazaretto
libretto	stiletto		

ETTY, ETI, ETTI

Betty	fretty	Hetty	jetty
Letty	petty	sweaty	confetti
spaghetti	spermacetti		

EUDAL (*see* OODLE)   EUTER (*see* OOTER)

EVEL

bevel	devil	Greville	level
Neville	revel	dishevel	

EVER (*short*)

clever	ever	never	sever
Trevor	assever	dissever	endeavour
however	whatever	whenever	wherever
whoever	(*For* EVER, *as in "fever," see* EAVER.)		

EVEREST

Everest	cleverest	severest

EVIL

evil	weevil	coeval	primeval
medieval			

EVIOUS

devious	previous

EVY (*see* EAVY)

EWAGE

brewage	"New Age"	sewage	escuage

EWARD, EWERED

leeward   Seward   steward   sewered
skewered

EWEL, UEL

crewel   cruel   dual   duel
Ewell   fuel   gruel   jewel
ruelle   (*Compare* OOL *and* ULE.)

EWER

bluer	booer	brewer	chewer
Clewer	cooer	doer	fewer
hewer	newer	scrêwer	sewer
skewer	strewer	truer	twoer
viewer	wooer	construer	interviewer
pursuer	renewer	reviewer	

(*And compare* OOR *and* URE.)

EWESS

Jewess   Lewes   Lewis   U.S.
St. Louis

EWISH

blueish   Jewish   shrewish   twoish

EWTER, EUTER, UTER, UTOR

Ceuta   muter   neuter   pewter
suitor   tutor   disputer

(*And further extensions in* UTE. *Compare* OOTER.)

EWY, OUE, UEY

bluey   coo-ee   Coué   dewy
gluey   Jewy   Louie   roué

EXILE

exile   flexile

EXION (*see* ECTION)

EXOR, EXER

flexor   (*And extend* EX.)

EXTANT

extant   sextant

EXTILE

sextile   textile

EXY

sexy   apoplexy

EYANCE, EANCE

| seance | abeyance | conveyance | purveyance |

IAD

| dryad | naiad | hamadryad | jeremiad |

IAL, IOL

dial	Dyall	phial	Lyell
trial	vial	viol	decrial
denial	retrial	(*Compare* ILE *in one-syllable list.*)	

IAN (*see* EON)

IANCE, IENCE

| science | affiance | alliance | appliance |
| compliance | defiance | reliance | |

IANT, IENT

| Bryant | client | giant | pliant |
| compliant | defiant | reliant | self-reliant |

166

IAR

briar	brier	buyer	drier
Dwyer	dyer	friar	fryer
higher	liar	Maria	nigher
plier	prior	pryer	skier
spryer			

(See under Y in one-syllable rhymes for further extensions in Y and IGH. Compare IRE.)

IAS

bias	pious	Ananias	nisi-prius

IAT, IET, IOT

diet	fiat	quiet	riot
ryot	striate	Wyatt	disquiet

IBALD

ribald   *(Extend IBBLE for "quibbled," etc.)*

IBBER

fibber   wine-bibber

(Extend IB for "cribber," etc.)

IBBET, IBIT

gibbet	Tibbett	cohibit	exhibit
inhibit	prohibit		

IBBLE

cribble	dibble	dribble	fribble
nibble	quibble	Ribble	scribble
Sybil			

IBBON

gibbon	ribbon

IBER

fiber	Khyber	Tiber

(And extend IBE for "inscriber," etc.)

IBLE, IBAL
Bible   libel   tribal

IBLET
driblet   giblet   triblet

ICAR   ICKER
bicker   liquor   vicar   (*And extend* ICK.)

ICHEN
lichen   Hitchin   kitchen

ICHES, ITCHES, EECHES
breeches   riches   (*And extend* ITCH.)

ICIAN, ICION, ITION, ISSION

mission	abolition	academician	acquisition
addition	admission	admonition	ambition
ammunition	apparition	apposition	arithmetician
attrition	audition	circuition	circumcision
circumposition	coalition	cognition	coition
commission	competition	composition	condition
contraposition	contrition	decomposition	definition
demolition	dentition	deposition	disparition
disquisition	ebullition	edition	electrician
emission	emolition	erudition	exhibition
expedition	exposition	fruition	geometrician
ignition	imposition	inanition	indisposition
inhibition	inquisition	insition	intermission
interposition	intromission	intuition	juxtaposition
logician	magician	malnutrition	manumission
mathematician	mechanician	metaphysician	monition
munition	musician	nutrition	omission
opposition	optician	partition	parturition
patrician	perdition	permission	petition
physician	politician	position	precognition
predisposition	premonition	preposition	presupposition
preterition	prodition	prohibition	proposition
readmission	recognition	recommission	recomposition
reddition	remission	rendition	repetition

168

reposition	requisition	rhetorician	sedition
submission	superstition	supposition	suspicion
transition	transmission	transposition	tuition
volition			

ICIOUS, ITIOUS

vicious	adventitious	ambitious	auspicious
avaricious	capricious	cilicious	delicious
factitious	fictitious	flagitious	ignitious
inauspicious	injudicious	judicious	malicious
Mauritius	meretricious	nutritious	officious
pernicious	propitious	seditious	superstitious
supposititious	surreptitious	suspicious	unsuspicious

ICKEN

| chicken | quicken | sicken | stricken |
| thicken | wicken | | |

ICKENING

strychnine   (*And extend words in previous list.*)

ICKER (*see* ICAR)

ICKET

clicket	cricket	picket	piquet
pricket	snicket	spicate	thicket
ticket	wicket	intricate	

(*And pluralize some words in this list for "rickets."*)

ICKLE, ICKEL

fickle	mickle	nickel	pickle
prickle	sickle	stickle	strickle
tickle	trickle		

ICKLY

| quickly | prickly | sickly | slickly |
| thickly | | | |

169

ICKSHAW

kickshaw   rickshaw

ICKY

Vicky   *(And extend* ICK *for "bricky," etc.)*

ICTER, ICTOR

lictor	victor	Victor	boa-constrictor

ICTION, IXION

diction	fiction	friction	addiction
adstriction	affixion	affliction	affriction
astriction	benediction	commixion	constriction
contradiction	conviction	crucifixion	dereliction
eviction	indiction	infliction	interdiction
jurisdiction	malediction	obstriction	prediction
prefixion	restriction	reviction	valediction

ICTURE

picture   stricture   *(And see* IXTURE.)

ICY

icy   spicy

IDAL, IDLE, IDOL

bridal	bridle	idle	idol
idyll	sidle	tidal	fratricidal
homicidal	parricidal	regicidal	suicidal

IDAY *(see* IDY)

IDDEN

bidden	chidden	hidden	midden
ridden	forbidden	unbidden	

IDDISH

kiddish   Yiddish

IDDLE
diddle	fiddle	griddle	middle
piddle	riddle	twiddle	tarradiddle

IDDY
Biddy	giddy	kiddie	middy
skiddy			

IDEN, IDON
guidon	Sidon	widen

IDENT
guidant	strident	trident	dividant

IDEOUS
hideous	fastidious	insidious	invidious
lapidious	perfidious		

IDER
cider	Ida	spider	(*And extend* IDE.)

IDGET, IGIT
Bridget	digit	fidget	midget

IDGY   IDLE (*see* IDAL)
midgy	ridgy

IDLY, IDELY
idly	widely

IDY, IDAY
Friday	sidy	tidy	bona-fide

IEFLY
briefly	chiefly

IENCE (*see* IANCE)   IESTLY (*see* EASTLY)   IET (*see* IAT)

IFER, IPHER

cipher	fifer	lifer	rifer
decipher			

IFFER

biffer	differ	sniffer

IFFIN

Biffen	griffin	tiffin

IFFLE

piffle	whiffle

IFFY

jiffy	Liffy	niffy	sniffy
squiffy	whiffy		

IFIC

beatific	calorific	hieroglyphic	horrific
pacific	prolific	rubific	scientific
sensific	semnific	soporific	specific
terrific			

IFLE

eyeful	rifle	stifle	trifle

IFTER

drifter	lifter	shifter	sifter
snifter	swifter	shop-lifter	

IFTY

drifty	fifty	"giftie"	nifty
shifty	thrifty		

IGATE (*see* IGOT)

IGEON, IDGEON

pigeon	Phrygian	Stygian	widgeon
religion	irreligion		

IGER

Niger   Riga   tiger

IGEST

digest (*noun*)   obligest

IGGARD, IGGERED, IGURD

figured   niggard   (*And extend* **IGGER**.)

IGGER, IGOR, IGURE

bigger   digger   figure   jigger
nigger   rigger   rigor   snigger
swigger   trigger   vigor   configure
disfigure   outrigger   transfigure

IGGIN

biggin   piggin

IGGISH

riggish   (*And extend* **IG**.)

IGGLE

giggle   higgle   niggle   sniggle
squiggle   wriggle

IGGY

iggy   piggy   twiggy

IGHER (*see* IAR)

IGHLAND

highland   island

IGHTEN, ITEN

Brighton   Crichton   triton
    (*And extend* **ITE** *and* **IGHT**.)

173

IGHTER, ITER

miter   niter
    (And extend ITE, IGHT *and* ITE *for* "smiter," "tighter,"
        "triter," *etc.)*

IGHTLY

sprightly   *(And extend* ITE *and* IGHT.*)*

IGHTNING

lightning
    (And extend IGHTEN *and* ITEN *for* ' tightening," "whit-
        ening," *etc.)*

IGHTY

Blighty	Clytie	flighty	mighty
mitey	nightie	whitey	almighty
Aphrodite			

IGIL

sigil   vigil

IGLY, IGGLY

bigly   giggly   sniggly   wriggly

IGMA

stigma   enigma

IGMENT

figment   pigment

IGOT, IGATE

bigot   frigate   gigot   spigot

IGOUR *(see* IGGER**)**

174

IGRESS

digress   tigress

IKEN, ICON

Dicon   icon   liken

IKING

Viking   (*And extend* IKE *for* "hiking," *etc.*)

IKY

Ikey   crikey   Psyche   spiky

ILACS, ILAX

lilacs   smilax

ILBERT

filbert   Gilbert

ILDER

builder   gilder   guilder   Hilda
bewilder   Matilda   St. Kilda

ILDISH

childish   mildish   wildish

ILFUL

skilful   wilful

ILIOUS

bilious   antrabilious   punctilious   supercilious

ILIGHT

highlight   skylight   stylite   twilight

ILKY

milky   silky   Willkie

ILLA

| Scylla | villa | chinchilla | gorilla |
| Manila | sarsaparilla | vanilla | |

ILLAGE

| billage | pillage | tillage | village |

ILLAR

pillar   caterpillar
  (*And extend* **ILL** *for "thriller," etc.*)

ILLET

| billet | fillet | millet | quillet |
| rillet | skillet | Willett | |

ILLIANT

brilliant   resilient

ILLIARDS

| billiards | chiliads | iliads | milliards |
| mill-yards | | | |

ILLING

shilling   (*And extend* **ILL** *for "drilling," etc.*)

ILLION, ILLIAN

billion	Chilean	Gillian	Lillian
million	pillion	trillion	carillon
Castilian	civilian	cotillion	pavilion
postillion	reptilian	vermilion	

ILLOW

| billow | kilo | pillow | willow |
| armadillo | peccadillo | | |

176

ILLY

billy	Billy	Chile	filly
frilly	gillie	hilly	lily
Lillie	Milly	Scilly	silly
skilly	Willie	Piccadilly	

(*And extend* ILL *for "hilly," etc.*)

ILOM

whilom   asylum

ILTER

filter	gilter	jilter	lilter
milter	philter	quilter	tilter
wilter			

ILY, IGHLY

Filey   O'Reilly

(*And extend* Y *and* IGH *for "slily," "highly," etc.*)

IMAGE

image   scrimmage

IMATE

climate   primate

IMBER

limber   timber   unlimber

IMBLE, YMBAL

cymbal	gimble (*Lewis*	nimble	symbol
thimble	tymbal *Carroll*)	wimble	

IMBO

limbo   akimbo

IMER

climber   (*And extend* IME *for "primer," etc.*)

177

IMIC
chymic   mimic   patronymic

IMON, YMAN
flyman   pieman   Simon   Timon

IMMY
Jimmy   shimmy

IMPER
simper   (*And extend* IMP *for "shrimper," etc.*)

IMPLE
crimple   dimple   pimple   rimple
simple   wimple

IMSY
flimsy   "mimsy" (*Lewis Carroll*)   whimsy

IMUS
High Mass   primus   thymus   timous

IMY
blimey   grimy   limy   rimy
slimy   thymy   stymie   "gorblimey"

INA
china   Dinah   Carolina   regina
                (*Compare* INER)

INAL
final   spinal   trinal

INCERS
mincers   pincers   rinses

INCEST
incest   (*And extend* INCE *for "wincest," etc.*)

178

INCHER
clincher   flincher   pincher

INCTURE
cincture   tincture   vincture

INDER (*short*)
cinder   hinder   tinder

INDER (*long*) (*Extend* IND *for* "blinder," *etc.*)

INDLE
brindle   dwindle   **Hindle**   kindle
spindle   swindle   windle   rekindle

INDNESS
(*Extend* IND *as in* "kindness.")

INDY
Lindy   shindy   windy

INEAR, INNIER
linear   finnier   skinnier   whinnier

INER, INOR
minor (*And extend* INE *and* IGN *for* "finer," "assigner," *etc.*)
(*Compare* INA.)

INET
ginnet   linnet   minute   spinet

INEW, INUE
sinew   continue   discontinue

179

INFUL

sinful   skinful

INGENT

stringent   astringent   contingent   restringent

INGER

finger   linger   (*And extend* ING *for* "singer," *etc.*)

INGER   (*soft* "g")

ginger   injure   (*And extend* INGE *for* "cringer," *etc.*)

INGLE

cingle   cringle   dingle   ingle
jingle   mingle   shingle   single
springall   swingle   tingle   surcingle

INGLET

kinglet   ringlet   singlet

INGO

dingo   gringo   lingo   stingo
flamingo   jingo   Domingo

INGY

cringy   dingy   fringy   mingy
stingy   twingy

INIC

actinic   cynic   clinic

INGY   (*with hard* "g")

dinghy   springy   stringy

INION, INIAN

| Binyon | minion | Ninian | pinion |
| Carthaginian | dominion | opinion | Virginian |

INIS

| finis | Guinness | | |

INISH (*short*)

| finish | Finnish | thinnish | diminish |

INISH (*long*)

| brinish | nineish | swinish | |

INKLE

| crinkle | sprinkle | tinkle | twinkle |
| winkle | wrinkle | besprinkle | periwinkle |

INKLING *and* INKY (*extend* INK)

| Helsinki | dinky | slinky | |

INNER

| Pinner | (*And extend* IN *for* "dinner," *etc.*) | | |

INNOW

| minnow | winnow | | |

INNY

finny	guinea	Minnie	ninny
pinny	skinny	spinney	tinny
whinny	Winnie	ignominy	New Guinea

INO

| lino | rhino | | |

INSTER

| Leinster | minster | Minster | spinster |

181

INSY, INTAGE

linsey   quinsy   mintage   vintage

INTEL

lintel   quintal   pintle

INTER

winter   (*And extend* INT *for* "sprinter," *etc.*)

INTRY

vintry   wintry

INTY

flinty   minty   squinty   pepperminty

INUS

minus   sinus   spinous   vinous

INY

briny   liny   miny   piney
shiny   spiny   tiny   twiny
winy

ION

Brian   iron   lion   Lyon
scion   Zion   orion   dandelion

IPED

biped   strip*ed*   typ*ed*   **wip*ed***

IPEND

ripened   stipend

IPER, YPER

viper   (*And extend* IPE, YPE *for* "wiper," "typer," *etc.*)

IPHON, YPHEN
siphon   hyphen

IPIST, IPEST
typist   (*And extend* IPE *for* "*wipest,*" *etc.*)

IPPLE
cripple   nipple   ripple   stipple
tipple   triple

IPLING, IPPLING
Kipling   stripling
     (*And extend* IPPLE *for* "*rippling,*" *etc.*)

IPPER, IPPY
kipper   skipper
     (*And extend* IP *for* "*clipper,*" "*chippy,*" *etc.*)

IPPET
sippet   snippet   tippet   whippet

IPSTER
tipster   whipster

IPSY
gipsy   "ipse"   tipsy

IPTIC
cryptic   styptic   ecliptic   elliptic

IQUANT
piquant   secant   intersecant

IRANT
tyrant   virant   aspirant   conspirant

183

IRATE

gyrate   irate   pirate

IRCHEN, URCHIN

birchen   urchin

IRDAR, IRDER, ERDER, URDER

girder   herder   murder   sirdar
absurder

IRDLE, URDLE

curdle   girdle   hurdle

IRDLY

curdly   thirdly   absurdly

IREN

Byron   siren   syren

IRKIN (*see* ERKIN)

IRLING, ERLING, EARLING, URLING

sterling   Stirling   yearling   **whirling**
   (*And extend* EARL, IRL, URL.)

IRLISH, URLISH

churlish   girlish

IRLOIN

purloin   sirloin

184

IRMER, ERMER, URMUR

murmur   (*And extend* IRM *for "firmer," etc.*)

IRMISH

firmish   skirmish   squirmish

IRRAH

mirror   sirrah

IRREL

Birrel   Cyril   squirrel   Tyrrell
Tyrol   virile

IRRUP

chirrup   stirrup   syrup

IRTLE, URTLE

hurtle   kirtle   myrtle   Myrtle
spirtle   turtle

IRTY, URTY

Bertie   dirty   flirty   Gertie
shirty   skirty   spurty   squirty
thirty

IRUS

virus   desirous

IRY, IARY, IERY

briery   diary   fiery   miry
priory   spiry   wiry   enquiry

ISCARD

discard   Liscard

ISCOUNT

discount   miscount

ISCUIT (*see* ISKET)

ISCUS

discus   viscous

ISECT

bisect   trisect

ISER, ISOR

Kaiser   miser   sizar   visor
incisor   (*And extend* ISE *for "advisor," etc.*)

ISHER, ISSURE

disher   fisher   fissure   wisher

ISHOP

bishop   fish-shop

ISIC

Chiswick   phthisic   physic   metaphysic

ISION, ISSION

scission	vision	abscission	allision
circumcision	collision	decision	derision
division	ellision	Elysian	excision
incision	misprision	precision	prevision
provision	recision	rescission	revision
subdivision	television		

(*For rhymes to "mission" see* ICIAN.)

ISIS

crisis   Isis   phthisis

(And compare plurals of ICE.*)*

ISIT

visit   exquisite

ISKER

brisker   frisker   risker   whisker

ISKET

biscuit   brisket   wisket

ISKY

frisky   risky   whisky

ISLY, IZZLY

Bisley   drizzly   frizzly   grisly
grizzly

ISMAL

dismal   abysmal   baptismal

ISON (*see* IZZEN)

ISPER

crisper   lisper   whisper

ISSAL (*see* ISTLE)   ISSION (*see* ICIAN)

ISSUE

issue   fichu   tissue   atishoo

ISSURE (*see* ISHER)

ISTANCE

distance	assistance	co-existence	consistence
equidistance	existence	inconsistence	insistence
non-existence	non-resistance	resistance	subsistence

ISTANT (*adapt previous list for "distant," etc.*)

ISTEN

christen	glisten	listen

ISTER

bister	blister	glister	mister
sister	twister		

ISTHMUS (*see* ISTMAS)

ISTIC

cystic	fistic	mystic	anarchistic
atheistic	bolshevistic	cabalistic	characteristic
communistic	deistic	fascistic	pantheistic
polytheistic	socialistic	syllogistic	theistic
tritheistic			

ISTINE

Christine	pristine	amethystine

ISTLE, ISSAL

bristle	gristle	missal	missel
missile	thistle	whistle	dismissal
epistle			

ISTMAS

Christmas	isthmus

ISTOL

Bristol	crystal	pistol

ITAL

title	vital	entitle	marital
recital	requital	subtitle	

ITER

miter	niter

(*And extend* ITE *and* IGHT *for* "biter," "lighter," *etc.*)

ITHER (*short*)

blither	dither	hither	slither
thither	whither	wither	zither

ITHER (*long*) (*see* EITHER *with* "*i*" *sounded*)

ITIAN

titian	(*And see rhymes in* ICIAN. *Compare* ISION.)

ITIC

critic	hypercritic	hypocritic	mephitic
politic	syphilitic		

ITISH, ITTISH

British	fittish	kittish	skittish

ITNESS

fitness	witness

ITTANCE

pittance	(*And extend* IT *for* "quittance," "admittance," *etc.*)

ITTED, ITIED
(*Extend* IT *and* ITTY *for* "pitted," "pitied," *etc.*)

ITTEN

bitten	Briton	kitten	mitten
smitten	Witan	written	Thames Ditton

ITTER

bitter	"crittur"	fitter	flitter
fritter	glitter	hitter	knitter
litter	pitter	quitter	sitter
slitter	spitter	splitter	titter
twitter	(*And extend* IT *for* "transmitter," *etc.*)		

ITTLE, ITTAL, ICTUAL

brittle	knittle	little	quittal
skittle	spittle	tittle	victual
whittle	wittol	acquittal	belittle
committal	transmittal		

ITTY

chitty	city	ditty	gritty
Kitty	nitty	pity	pretty
witty	banditti	committee	

ITUAL

ritual	habitual

IVAL

rival	(*And extend* IVE *for* "arrival," *etc.*)

IVEL, IVIL

civil	drivel	rivel	shrivel
snivel	swivel	uncivil	

IVEN

driven	given	riven	shriven
striven	wivern		

IVER (*short*)

"flivver"	giver	liver	quiver
river	shiver	sliver	deliver
Guadalquivir			

IVER (*long*)

fiver	Ivor	stiver	saliva
Lady Godiva			

(*And extend* IVE *for* "diver," *etc.*)

IVET, IVIT

civet	privet	rivet	trivet
Glenlivet	(*Compare* IVOT.)		

IVID

chivvied	livid	vivid

IVOT

divot	pivot	(*Compare* IVET.)

IVY (*short*)

civvy	chivy	Livy	privy
skivvy	tantivy	(*No rhyme for* "ivy.")	

IXIE

dixie	Dixie	pixy	tricksy
Trixie			

IXER, IXIR

elixir   (*And extend* IX *for* "fixer," *etc.*)

IXTURE

fixture	mixture	admixture	commixture

IZARD, IZZARD, ISSORED

bizard	blizzard	gizzard	Izzard
lizard	scissored	vizard	wizard

IZZEN, IZEN, ISON

mizzen	prison	wizen	bedizen
imprison	(*Compare* ISTEN.)		

IZON *and* ISON (*long*)

bison	horizon

IZZIER

busier	dizzier	fizzier	frizzier
vizier			

IZZLE

chisel	drizzle	fizzle	frizzle
grizzle	mizzle	sizzle	

IZZLING

quisling (*And extend above as in* "*drizzling.*")

IZZY, USY

busy	dizzy	fizzy	frizzy
Lizzie	mizzy	tizzy	

OA

boa	Goa	moa	Noah
poa	proa	Genoa	Iowa
jerboa	Samoa		

OADER, ODOR

odor
 (*And extend* OAD, ODE *for* "*loader*," "*exploder*," *etc.*)
 (*Compare* ODA.)

OAFY

feoffee	loafy	oafy	Sophie
strophe	trophy		

OAKER, OKER, OCHRE

ochre   Roker

(And extend OAK *and* OKE *for "soaker," "joker," etc.)*

OAKUM, OCUM

hokum	locum	oakum	Slocum

OALY, OLY, OLEY, OLLY (*long*), OWLY

coaly	Crowley	drolly	goalie
holey	holy	lowly	moly
Rowley	shoaly	slowly	wholly
roly-poly			

OAMER

comber	Cromer	foamer	Homer
omer	roamer	misnomer	

(Compare OMA.)

OANER, ONER, ONOR, OWNER

donor	loaner	loner	moaner
Mona	owner	postponer	stoner
atoner	Corona	deponer	intoner
telephoner	Arizona	*(Compare* ONA)	

OAPY

mopy	soapy	topee

OARISH

boarish	whorish	*(Compare* OORISH.)

OARSER

coarser	courser	forcer	hawser
hoarser			

(Compare AUCER.)

OARY, ORY

dory	glory	gory	hoary
lory	more (*Latin*)	storey	story
Tory	furore		

OASTAL, OSTAL

coastal   postal

OASTER, OSTER (*Extend* OAST *and* OST *for* "coaster," "poster," *etc.*)

OATBRIDGE

boat-bridge   Coatbridge   moat-bridge

OATER, OTER, OTOR

bloater   motor   (*And extend* OAT *and* OTE.)
   (*Compare* OTA.)

OBBER

clobber	slobber	swabber	(*And extend* OB.)

OBBIN

bobbin	Dobbin	robin	Robin

OBBLE

cobble	gobble	hobble	nobble
squabble	wobble	(*Add* "r" *for* "cobbler," *etc.*)	

OBBY

bobby	Bobby	hobby	knobby
lobby	mobby	nobby	Robbie

OBELESS, OBLESSE

noblesse   robeless

OBER

prober   rober   sober   October

OBOE

hobo   oboe   Launcelot Gobbo (*"Merchant*
                                              of Venice")

OCAL

focal   local   phocal   vocal

OCEAN (*see* OTION)

OCER, OSER, OSSER

closer   grocer   engrosser   (*Extend* OSE.)

OCHRE (*see* OAKER)

OCKADE

blockade   brocade   cockade   **dock-aid**
okayed   stockade

OCKER

cocker   soccer   knickerbocker
(*And extend* OCK *for "shocker," etc.*)

OCKET

brocket   docket   locket   **pocket**
rocket   socket   sprocket   **pickpocket**

OCKNEY

cockney   **knock-knee**

OCKY

cocky   crocky   hockey   **jockey**
rocky   stocky

195

OCOA, OCO, OKO

boko   cocoa   toko   Orinoco
rococo

OCTION (see AUCTION)

OCTOR

doctor   proctor   concocter   decocter

OCUM (see OAKUM)

OCUS

crocus   focus   hocus   locus
trochus   hocus-pocus

OCUST

focused   hocused   locust

ODA

coda   Rhoda   soda   Baroda
pagoda   Fashoda   (*Compare* OADER.)

ODDEN

Flodden   sodden   trodden   untrodden

ODDER

codder   dodder   fodder   nodder
odder   plodder   prodder

ODDESS, ODICE

bodice   goddess

196

ODDEST, ODEST

bodiced   modest   (*And extend* ODD *for "oddest," etc.*)

ODDLE, ODEL

coddle	model	noddle	swaddle
toddle	waddle	yodel	

ODDY, ODY

body	cloddy	noddy	shoddy
toddy	busybody	embody	Irrawaddy
Tom Noddy			

ODGER

dodger	codger	lodger	stodger

ODGY

podgy	splodgy	stodgy

ODIC

odic	episodic	periodic	spasmodic
synodic			

ODIUM

odium	podium	sodium	allodium

ODOR (*see* OADER)

ODUS

modus	nodus

OEM, OET

poem	proem	poet	inchoate

OEY

blowy	Bowie	Chloe	doughy
goey	Joey	snowy	showy

OFA

chauffeur	gopher	loafer	sofa

OFFEE

coffee	toffee

OFFER

coffer	cougher	doffer	golfer
offer	proffer	scoffer	

OFTEN, OFTENER

often	soften	oftener	softener

OFTY

lofty	softy

OGEY

bogey	fogey	Yogi

OGGISH

doggish	froggish	hoggish

OGGLE

boggle	coggle	goggle	joggle
toggle			

OGGY

boggy	cloggy	doggy	foggy
froggie	groggy	joggy	moggie
soggy			

OGLE

bogle	ogle

OGRESS

ogress	progress

OIC

stoic	heroic	azoic	diapnoic

OIDER

moider	avoider	embroider

OILY

coyly	doily	oily

(Compare "loyally" and "royally.")

OINER

coiner	joiner	purloiner	Moyna

OINTMENT

ointment   *(And extend* OINT.)

OISTER, OYSTER

cloister	foister	hoister	moister
oyster	roister		

OITER

goiter	loiter	Ruyter	adroiter
exploiter			

OKAY

bouquet	okay	Tokay	Touquet

OKEN, OAKEN

token	betoken	*(And extend* OAK *and* OKE.)

OKEY

chokey	croquet	joky	oaky
poky	smoky	trochee	

OLAR, OLLER, OWLER

bowler	droller	molar	polar
roller	solar	stroller	toller
comptroller	condoler	consoler	controller
enroller			

OLDEN

golden	olden	beholden	embolden

OLDER, OULDER

boulder   molder   shoulder   smolder
(*And extend* OLD *for "folder," etc.*)

OLEFUL

bowlful   doleful   soulful

OLEMN, OLUMN

column   solemn

OLEN, OLON

colon   Nolan   solen   solon
stolen   swollen   semi-colon

OLIC, OLLICK

colic   frolic   rollick   alcoholic
apostolic   bucolic   carbolic   diabolic
hyperbolic   melancholic   parabolic   vitriolic
(*Compare* AULIC.)

OLID

dollied   jollied   solid   squalid
stolid   volleyed

OLISH, OLLISH

dollish   polish   abolish   demolish

OLIUM

scholium   linoleum   petroleum

OLLAR, OLAR, OLER

choler   collar   dollar   dolor
scholar   squalor   Waller

OLLARD, OLLARED

bollard   collared   dollared   Lollard
pollard   "scholard"

OLLEGE, OWLEDGE

college   knowledge   acknowledge

OLLET

collet   wallet

OLLIER

collier   jollier

OLLOP

collop	dollop	gollop	lollop
scollop	trollop	wallop	

OLLOW

follow	hollow	Rollo	swallow
wallow	Apollo		

OLLY, OLLEY

brolly	collie	dolly	Dolly
folly	golly	holly	jolly
Molly	Polly	Solly	trolley
volley	melancholy		

OLO

bolo   polo   solo

OLSTER

bolster   holster   oldster   upholster

OLORED

colored   dullard

OLTER, OULTER

bolter	colter	jolter	molter
poulter	revolter		

OLTEST, OULTICED

poulticed   *(And extend* OLT *for "joltest," etc.)*

OLTISH
coltish   doltish

OLUMN (*see* OLEMN)   OLY (*see* OALY)

OMA
coma	soma	Roma	aboma
aroma	diploma	Tacoma	

(*Compare* OAMER.)

OMACH, UMMOCK
hummock   stomach (*Add "s" to rhyme with "flummox."*)

OMAIN
domain   ptomaine

OMAN, OWMAN
bowman	foeman	gnomon	Roman
showman	snow-man	yeoman	

OMBAT
combat   wombat

OMBER
bomber   omber   somber

OMEN
omen   (*And pluralise words under* OMAN; *thus "bowmen."*)

OMENT
foment (*noun*)   loment   moment

OMET, OMIT
comet   vomit   Mahomet

OMIC

comic   atomic   astronomic   econcmic
gnomic

OMING, UMBING, UMMING

coming   plumbing
(*And extend* UM *for "humming," etc.*)

OMMY

Tommy   bonhomie   consommé   Dahomey

OMPASS

compass   rumpus   encompass

OMPTER

compter   prompter   accompter

ONA

donar   Jonah   Mona   Arizona
Catriona   corona   Cremona   Iona
Verona   (*Compare* OANER.)

ONAGE

nonage   Swanage

ONDANT, ONDENT

fondant   despondent   correspondent   respondent

ONDEL, ONDLE

Blondel   fondle   rondle   Wandle

ONDER

blonder   bonder   condor   fonder
ponder   squander   wander   yonder
(*Extend* OND *for "absconder," etc.*)

ONELY

lonely   only

ONEST

connest   donnest   honest   wannest
non est

ONGER

conger   longer   stronger   Tonga
wronger

ONGO

Congo   pongo

ONIC

chronic	conic	tonic	adonic
alcyonic	Byronic	carbonic	diatonic
embryonic	euphonic	gramophonic	harmonic
histrionic	ionic	ironic	laconic
macaronic	microphonic	mnemonic	platonic
Slavonic	symphonic	telephonic	Teutonic

ONION (*see* UNION)

ONISH, ONNISH

donnish   admonish   astonish   premonish

ONKY, ONKEY

conky   donkey   wonky

ONKEY (*as in* "monkey," *see* UNKY)

ONNAGE, UNNAGE

dunnage   Dunwich   tonnage

ONNET

bonnet   sonnet

204

ONNY

| bonny | Johnny | Connie | nonny |
| Ronnie | | | |

ONOR, ONER

| goner | honor | wanner | dishonor |

ONSIL, ONSUL

| consul | sponsal | tonsil | proconsul |
| responsal · | | | |

ONTEST, ONTRACT

| contest | wantest | contract | entr'acte |

ONY, ONEY

bony	cony	coney	crony
drony	phoney	pony	stony
tony	Tony	boloney	macaroni
Marconi	polony		

ONYX

| onyx | phonics | | |

OOBY

| booby | looby | ruby | Ruby |

OODLE

boodle	feudal	noodle	poodle
doodle	caboodle	canoodle	flapdoodle
Yankee-Doodle			

OODY (*short*)

| goodie | roody | woody | |

OODY (*long*)

broody   Judy   moody

OOKISH

bookish   flukish   rookish   spookish

OOKY (*short*)

bookie   cookie   hookey   rookie

OOKY (*long*)

fluky   spooky   Sukie

OOLISH, ULISH, OOMY, UMY (*extend* OOL, ULE, OOM *and* UME)

OONER (*see* UNAR)   OONFUL (*see* UNEFUL)

OONY, UNY

pruny   puisne   puny   tuny
      (*And extend* OON *for "loony," etc.*)

OOPER, UPER, UPOR

Cupar   super   stupor
      (*And extend* OOP *for "cooper," etc.*)

OOPY, OUPY

croupy   droopy   loopy   rupee
soupy   whoopee   whoopy

OORISH

boorish   Moorish   poorish

OOSER, USER
(*Extend* OOSE *and* USE, *etc., for* "chooser," "bruiser,"
"loser," "user," *etc.*)

OOTER

freebooter
(*And extend* OOT *for* "hooter," *etc. Compare* EWTER.)

OOTLE

Bootle   brutal   footle   tootle
refutal

OOTY

beauty   booty   cutie   dhooti
duty   fluty   fruity   rooty
sooty

OOVER

groover   prover   maneuver   Vancouver
(*And extend* OOVE *and* OVE *for* "hoover," "remover,"
etc.)

OOZLE, OUSEL, USIL

foozle   fusil   ousel   bamboozle
perusal   refusal

OOZY

boozy   newsy   oozy

OPAL

Bhopal   copal   opal   Adrianople
Constantinople

207

OPER (short), OPPER

Dopper   Joppa   proper   improper
(And extend OP for "shopper," "topper," etc.)

OPER (long), OAPER

sloper   Soper   toper
(And extend OAP and OPE for "soaper," "moper," etc.)

OPHET

profit   prophet   Tophet

OPHIST

officed   sophist
(And extend OFF for "doffest," etc.)

OPIC

topic   tropic
(And extend OPE for "microscopic," etc.)

OPISH

mopish   Popish

OPLAR, OPLING

poplar   toppler   fopling   toppling

OPPY (short)

copy   Poppy   *(And extend OP for "floppy," etc.)*

OPSY

dropsy   topsy   Topsy   autopsy

208

OPTIC

Coptic   optic   synoptic

OPTION

option   adoption

OPY (*long*), OAPY

soapy   topee   (*And extend* OPE *for* "mopy," *etc.*)

ORA

aura	Cora	Dora	flora
Flora	Laura	Norah	Kiora
Andorra	Aurora		

(*And compare extensions of* OAR *and* ORE *as in* "roarer"
and "snorer.")

ORAGE

borage   forage   porridge

ORAL (*short*)

| coral | laurel | moral | quarrel |
| sorrel | Balmoral | immoral | unmoral |

ORAL (*long*)

| aural | choral | floral | horal |
| oral | thoral | binaural | femoral |

ORAN

Koran   moron

ORAX

borax   storax   thorax

ORBEL
bauble   corbel   warble

ORCHARD, ORCHER
orchard   tortured   lorcha   scorcher
torture

ORDER, OARDER
Cawdor   Lauder   order   warder
    (*And extend words under* OARD. *Thus "hoarder," "re-corder," etc.*)

ORDIAL, ORDEAL
cordial   ordeal   primordial

ORDLING
dawdling   lordling   maudlin

ORDON
Bordon   cordon   Gordon   Jordan
warden

ORDSHIP
lordship   wardship

OREAL, ORIAL
boreal   oriel   ambassadorial.   armorial
conspiratorial   dictatorial   equatorial   immemorial
inquisitorial   memorial   pictorial   senatorial

OREIGN, ORIN
foreign   florin   sporran   warren

ORELOCK
forelock   Porlock   warlock

ORENCE

| Florence | Lawrence | torrents | abhorrence |

OREST, ORIST

| forest | florist |

ORGAN

| gorgon | Morgan | organ | Glamorgan |

ORGER

| Borgia | forger | gorger | disgorger |

ORGI, ORGY

| Corgi | Georgie | orgy |

ORIC

choric	chloric	doric	Warwick
Yorrick	allegoric	categoric	historic
metaphoric	paregoric	prehistoric

ORID, ORRID

| forehead | florid | horrid | quarried |
| torrid |

ORIS

| Boris | Doris | Horace | loris |
| morris | Norris | deoch-an-doras | *(often misspelled as "dock and doris")* |

ORKY

| corky | door-key | porky |
| | *(Compare* AWKY.*)* |

ORMAL

| formal | normal | abnormal |

ORMAN

| doorman | foreman | Mormon | Norman |
| storeman | longshoreman |

211

ORMANT

dormant   torment   informant

ORMER

dormer   Walmer   warmer

(And extend ORM *for "former," etc.)*

ORNER

corner   Lorna   pawner   scorner
warner   yawner   suborner

(Compare OURNER.) *(Extend* AWN *for "spawner," etc.)*

ORNET

cornet   hornet

ORNING, AWNING

awning   mourning

(And extend AWN *and* ORN *for "dawning," "morning," etc.)*

ORNY

corny   horny   Pawnee   thorny

(Compare AWNY.)

OROUGH

borough   thorough   *(Compare* URROW)

ORPOR, AUPER

pauper   torpor   warper

ORPUS

corpus   porpoise   habeas corpus

ORRAL, ORREL *(see* ORAL, *short)*

212

ORRENT

torrent   warrant   abhorrent

ORRID (*see* ORID)

ORROR

horror   abhorrer

ORROW

borrow   morrow   Morro   sorrow

ORRY

Florrie   Laurie   lorry   quarry
soirée   sorry   (*For rhymes to "worry," see* URRY.)

ORSAL, ORSEL

dorsal   foresail   morsel   torsal

ORSET

corset   Dorset

ORSTED, IRSTED

thirsted   worsted

ORTAGE

cortege   portage

ORTAL, ORTLE

chortle   mortal   portal   tortile
aortal   immortal

213

ORTAR, ORTER

mortar   quarter
    (*Extend* ORT *for "porter," etc., and compare* AUGHTER.)

ORTEN

quarten   Morton   Norton   shorten
Wharton

ORTION

portion   torsion   abortion   apportion
    (*Extend* ORT *for "contortion," etc., and compare*
    AUTION.)

ORTLY, OURTLY

courtly   (*And extend* ORT *for "portly," etc.*)

ORTIVE

sportive   tortive   abortive

ORTRESS

court-dress   fortress   portress

ORTUNE

fortune   importune   misfortune

ORTURE (*see* ORCHER)

ORTY

forte   forty   porty   rorty
snorty   sortie   sporty   warty
    (*Compare* AUGHTY.)

214

ORUM

forum	jorum	quorum	Shoreham
ad valorem	cockalorem	decorum	indecorum
pons asinorum			

ORUS, AURUS

aurous	chorus	chlorous	porous
taurus	canorous	decorous	imporous
sonorous			

ORWAY   OSEN (*see* OZEN, *long*)

doorway   Norway

OSET, OSIT

closet	posit	posset	deposit

OSHER

cosher	Kosher	posher	swasher
washer			

OSIER, OSURE

cosier	crozier	dozier	hosier
osier	nosier	rosier	

(And extend OSE *for "closure," etc.)*

OSKY

bosky   drosky

OSMIC

cosmic   osmic

OSSACKS

Cossacks   Trossachs

OSSAGE

Osage   bossage   sausage

OSSER

bosser   dosser   ·   josser   prosser
tosser   embosser

OSSUM

blossom   oppossum

OSSY

Flossie   (*And extend* OSS *for* "*bossy,*" *etc.*)

OSTAL (*short*), OSTEL

costal   hostel   postil   pentecostal

OSTAL (*long*) (*see* OASTAL)

OSTER (*long*) (*see* OASTER)

OSTER (*short*)

coster   foster   Gloucester   accoster
paternoster

OSTESS

ghostess   hostess

OSTIC

caustic   gnostic   joss-stick   accostic
agnostic   diagnostic   prognostic

OSTLE, OSSIL

dossil   fossil   jostle   throstle
wassail   apostle

216

OSTLER

hostler   jostler   ostler   wassailer

OSTLY, OSTREL

ghostly   mostly   costrel   nostril

OSTRUM   OSURE (*see* OZIER)

nostrum   rostrum

OSY, OZY

cosy   dozy   nosy   posy
prosy   rosy   Rosie

OTA

quota   rota   Bogota   Dakota
iota   Minnesota   (*Compare* OATER.)

OTAL

dotal   total   anecdotal   antidotal
sacerdotal   teetotal

OTARD

dotard   motored

OTCHER

botcher   notcher   watcher   top-notcher

OTER, OTOR (*see* OATER)

OTHER

bother   pother

OTHER (*as in "mother"*)

brother	mother	smother	other
another	Anstruther		

OTIC

azotic	chaotic	despotic	erotic
exotic	hypnotic	idiotic	nepotic
patriotic	quixotic		

OTION, OCEAN

lotion	motion	notion	ocean
potion	commotion	devotion	emotion
locomotion	promotion		

OTIVE

motive	votive	locomotive

OTLY

hotly	motley	Otley	squatly

OTNESS

hotness	Totness

OTTAGE

cottage	pottage	wattage

OTTEN, OTTON

cotton	"hot 'un" (*And extend* OT *for "rotten," etc.*)

OTTER, OTA

ottar	otter	cottar	squatter
swatter	(*And extend* OT *for "hotter," etc.*)		

OTTISH

Scottish	schottische	sottish

218

OTTLE, OTTEL

bottle	dottel	mottle	pottle
throttle	wattle		

OTTO

blotto	grotto	motto	Otto
ridotto	Watteau	what ho!	

OTTY

Lottie   Totty   (*And extend* OT *for "dotty," etc.*)

OTUM, OTEM

pro tem   quotum   totem

OUBLE, UBBLE

bubble	double	rubble	stubble
trouble			

OUBLET

doublet   sub-let

OUCHER

coucher   poucher   voucher

OUDER (*see* OWDER)

OUGHTY (*see* AUGHTY *and* OUTY)

OUGHBOY   OUGHBOY (*with "o" sounded*)

cowboy   ploughboy   doughboy   hautboy

OULDER (*see* OLDER)   OUNDER (*extend* OUND)

OUNSEL

council   counsel   groundsel

OUNTAIN

fountain   mountain

OUNTY

bounty   county   "mounty" (*Canadian*)

OUNTER

encounter   rencounter
    (*And extend* OUNT *for* "*mounter,*" "*discounter,*" *etc.*)

OURAGE

borage   courage   demurrage   discourage
encourage

OURISH

currish   flourish   nourish

OURNEY, ERNY

Burney   Czerny   Ernie   ferny
journey   tourney   attorney

OUSAL

housel   tousle   carousal   espousal

OUSER (*see* OWSER)   OUSIN (*see* OZEN)

OUSY, OWZY

blowzy	drowsy	frowsy	lousy
mousy			

OUTY, OUGHTY

doughty	droughty	flouty	gouty
pouty	snouty	sprouty	

OVEL

grovel	hovel	novel

OVEL (*as in "shovel"*)

Lovel	shovel

OVEN (*short*)

covin	oven	sloven

OVEN (*long*)

cloven	proven	woven	interwoven

OVER (*short*)

cover	glover	lover	plover
shover	discover	recover	

OVER (*long*)

clover	Dover	drover	over
rover	stover	trover	moreover
half-seas-over			

OVETAIL

dovetail	love-tale

221

OWAGE
stowage   towage

OWARD, OWERED
coward   Howard (*And extend* OWER *for "flowered," etc.*)

OWDER, OUDER
chowder   crowder   louder   powder
prouder

OWDY
cloudy   dowdy   rowdy

OWEL
bowel   Powell   rowel   towel
trowel   vowel   disembowel   (*Compare* OWL.)

OWER (*as in "mower"*)
(Extend OW *and* OWE *for "crower," "ower," etc.*) **(Com-**
pare OUR.)

OWER (*as in "bower"*)
bower   cower   dower   flower
Giaour   lower   power   shower
tower   endower   overpower

OWLEDGE (*see* OLLEGE)

OWLER (*as in "bowler," see* OLAR)

OWLER, OULER
fouler   (*And extend* OWL *for "fowler," etc.*)

OWMAN (*see* OMAN)

OWNSMAN

gownsman   roundsman   townsman

OWNY, OWNIE

brownie   browny   downy   **Rowney**
towny

OWRY, OWERY, OURI

bowery   Bowery   cowry   dowry
floury   houri   (*And extend* OWER *for "flowery," etc.*)

OWSER

Bowser   browser   dowser   **grouser**
Mauser   mouser   rouser   towser
trouser   carouser   espouser

OWY

blowy   Chloe   doughy   **goey**
Joey   showy   snowy

OXEN

cockswain   oxen   Oxon

OXY

doxy   foxy   poxy   proxy
heterodoxy   orthodoxy

OYAL

loyal   royal   disloyal   (*Compare* OIL.)

223

OYANT

buoyant   clairvoyant

OYLY (*see* OILY)

OZEN (*short*), OUSIN

cousin   cozen   dozen

OZEN (*long*), OSEN

boatswain   chosen   frozen   squozen

OZZLE, OSEL

losel   nozzle   sozzle   schemozzle
schnozzle

UAL (*see* UEL)

UANT

fluent   truant   diluent   pursuant

UAVE

suave   Zouave

UBA

Cuba   tuba

UBBER

slubber   indiarubber   landlubber
(*And extend* UB *for* "rubber," *etc.*)

UBBERED

blubbered   cupboard   Hubbard   rubbered

UBBISH

cubbish   clubbish   grubbish   rubbish
tubbish

UBBLE (see OUBLE)

UBBLY

bubbly   doubly   knubbly   rubbly
stubbly

UBBY

cubby   chubby   grubby   hubby
scrubby   shrubby   stubby   tubby

UBIC

cubic   cherubic

UBLISH

bubblish   publish

UBY (see OOBY)   UCCOUR (see UCKER)

UCENT

lucent   recusant   reducent   translucent

UCID

deuced   loosed   lucid   mucid
pellucid

UCKER
succor   (*And extend* UCK *for* "mucker," *etc.*)

UCKET
bucket   tucket   Nantucket

UCKLE
buckle	chuckle	huckle	knuckle
muckle	stuckle	suckle	truckle
honeysuckle	unbuckle		

UCKLER
swashbuckler   (*And extend* UCKLE.)

UCKLING
duckling   (*And extend* UCKLE *for* "buckling," *etc.*)

UCKLED
cuckold   (*And extend* UCKLE *for* "buckled," *etc.*)

UCKY
ducky   Kentucky (*And extend* UCK *for* "mucky," *etc.*)

UCRE
eucher	fluker	lucre	snooker
rebuker			

UCTION, UXION
fluxion	ruction	suction	abduction
affluxion	construction	deduction	defluxion
destruction	effluxion	induction	instruction

introduction	misconstruction	obstruction	**production**
reduction	reproduction	seduction	superstruction
superinduction			

UDDER

"brudder"	dudder	flooder	**rudder**
scudder	shudder	udder	

UDDING

hooding	pudding	wooding

UDDLE

cuddle	fuddle	huddle	**muddle**
puddle	ruddle		

UDDY

bloody	buddy	cuddy	**muddy**
ruddy	studdy	study	

UDENT

prudent	student	concludent	imprudent

UDER, UDOR

Tudor	(*And extend* UDE *for "ruder," etc.*)

UDGEON

bludgeon	dudgeon	gudgeon	trudgeon
curmudgeon			

UDISH

blue-dish	crudish	dudish	lewdish
new dish	nudish	prudish	rudish
stew-dish			

UDIST

crudest	feudist	lewdest	nudest
nudist			

UEL

crewel	cruel	dual	duel
Ewell	fuel	gruel	jewel
renewal	ruelle	(*Compare* OOL *and* ULE.)	

UENT (*see* UANT)   UEY (*see* EWY)

UET

chuet	cruet	Hewett	suet

UFFER

buffer	duffer	suffer

(*And extend* UFF *and* OUGH.)

UFFIN

muffin	puffin	ragamuffin

UFFLE

buffel	duffel	muffle	ruffle
scuffle	shuffle	snuffle	truffle

UFFLY *and* UFFY (*extend* UFF *and* OUGH)

UFTY, UFTI

mufti	tufty

UGAL, UGLE

bugle	frugal	centrifugal	McDougall

UGGER

rugger	(*And extend* UG *for* "*lugger*," *etc.*)

UGGLE

| guggle | juggle | smuggle | snuggle |
| struggle | (*Add "r" for "juggler," etc.*) | | |

UGGY

| buggy | muggy | puggy | sluggy |

UGLY

| smugly | snugly | ugly | |

UICY

| goosey | juicy | Lucy | sluicy |
| Debussy | retroussé | | |

UID

| druid | fluid | | |

UIN

| bruin | ruin | Trewin | |

UISANCE

| nuisance | usance | | |

ULCER

| ulcer | repulser | | |

ULGAR

| Bulgar | fulgor | vulgar | |

ULGENT

| fulgent | effulgent | emulgent | indulgent |

ULKY

bulky   hulky   sulky

ULLAH

mullah   nullah   Abdulla (*Compare* ULLER.)

ULLARD

dullard   colored

ULLER, OLOR

color   culler   duller   sculler
discolor   medulla   (*Compare* ULLAH.)

ULLET (*as in "bullet"*)   ULLET (*as in "gullet"*)

bullet   pullet   gullet   mullet

ULLION

mullion   scullion   rapscallion

ULLY (*as in "fully"*)

bully   fully   pulley   woolly
   (*And many false rhymes in adverbs ending in* ULLY, *thus*
      "*beautifully.*")

ULLY (*as in "gully"*)

cully   dully   gully   hully
sully   Tully

ULPIT

bull-pit   pulpit

230

ULSION

compulsion	convulsion	emulsion	expulsion
impulsion	propulsion	repulsion	revulsion

ULSIVE (*adapt words in previous list for "impulsive," etc.*)

ULTRY

sultry   adult'ry

ULTURE

culture	multure	sculpture	vulture
agriculture	horticulture	sepulture	

ULU

Lulu   pulu   Zulu

ULY, UELY, EWLY, OOLIE, OOLY

bluely	coolie	coolly	duly
Julie	newly	ruly	truly
viewly	unduly	unruly	untruly

UMA

Duma   puma   Montezuma
    (*Compare* UMOR.)

UMAGE

fumage   plumage   roomage

UMAN

cueman	Crewe-man	crewman	human
Kew-man	Krooman	Newman	pew-man
woman	ichneumon	inhuman	

UMBAR, UMBER

cumber	Humber	lumbar	lumber
number	Rumba	slumber	umber
cucumber	encumber	outnumber	

UMBER (*soft "b"*), UMMER

comer	dumber	summer

(*And extend* UM *for "drummer," etc.*)

UMBLE

bumble	crumble	dumb-bell	fumble
grumble	humble	jumble	mumble
rumble	scumble	stumble	tumble

UMBLY, OMELY

comely	crumbly	dumbly	grumly
humbly	numbly		

(*Also Cholmondeley, pronounced "chumley."*)

UMBRIL

tumbril	umbril

UMID

fumid	humid	plum*ed*	tumid
exhum*ed*	perfum*ed*		

UMMIT

plummet	summit

UMMY

chummy	crummy	dummy	gummy
lummy	mummy	rummy	slummy
tummy			

UMOR, UMER, OOMER

bloomer	humor	rumor	stumer
tumor	(*And extend* OOM *and* UME.)		

UMOUS

fumous	glumous	grumous	humus
plumous	spumous	strumous	

UMPET

crumpet	strumpet	trumpet

UMPISH *and* UMPY (*extend* UMP)

UMPKIN

bumpkin	lumpkin	pumpkin

UMPLE

crumple	rumple

UMPTION

gumption	sumption	assumption	consumption
presumption	resumption		

UMPTIOUS

bumptious	gumptious	scrumptious	assumptious

UMPUS, OMPASS

compass	rumpus	encompass

UNAR, UNER, OONER

lunar	Poonah	schooner	Una
jejuner			

(*And* extend **OON**, **UNE**, *for* "crooner," "tuner," etc.)

UNBURNT

sunburnt	unburnt

UNCHEON

luncheon	nuncheon	puncheon	truncheon
Asuncion			

UNKLE

Funchal	truncal	uncle	carbuncle
siphuncle			

UNCTION

function	junction	unction	compunction
conjunction	defunction	disjunction	expunction
injunction	subjunction		

UNCTURE

juncture	puncture	conjuncture	compuncture

UNDAY, UNDY

Monday	Grundy (*Mrs.*)	Lundy	Sunday

UNDER

blunder	dunder	plunder	sunder
thunder	wonder	asunder	fecunder
jocunder	refunder	rotunder	thereinunder

UNDLE

| bundle | Blundell | rundle | trundle |

UNEFUL

| spoonful | tuneful |

UNGER (*soft "g"*)

| lunger | plunger | sponger | spunger |

UNGER (*hard "g"*)

| hunger | monger | younger | costermonger |
| fishmonger | ironmonger | | |

UNGLE

| bungle | jungle |

UNIC

| punic | Munich | runic | tunic |

UNION (*as in "bunion"*)

| bunion | Bunyan | onion | ronion |
| trunnion | | | |

UNION (*as in "union"*)

| union | communion | disunion | reunion |

UNIOR

| junior | punier | spoonier | tunier |

UNISH, UNNISH (*Extend* UN *for "punish," "Hunnish," etc.*)

UNKARD, UNKERED

bunkered   drunkard

UNKEN

drunken   Duncan   shrunken   sunken

UNKER

Junker   punkah   (*Extend* UNK *for* "bunker," *etc.*)

UNKET

junket   plunket

UNKY

flunkey	funky	hunky	monkey
nunky	spunky	trunky	

UNLIT

sunlit   unlit

UNNAGE

dunnage	Dunwich	Hun-age	nonage
tonnage			

UNNEL

funnel   gunwale   runnel   tunnel

UNSTER

Dunster   funster   Munster   punster

236

UNNY, ONY, ONEY

bunny	funny	honey	**money**
sonny	sunny	tunny	**acrimony**
agrimony	alimony	matrimony	

(And other false rhymes.)

UNTLE

frontal   disgruntle   contrapuntal

UPER, UPOR

Cupar   stupor   *(And see* **OOPER.***)*

UPID

Cupid   stupid

UPIL, UPLE

pupil   scruple   quadruple

UPPER

crupper   scupper   *(And extend* **UP** *for "supper," etc.)*

UPPLE

couple   supple

URAL

crural	mural	neural	**plural**
rural	Ural	intramural	

URANCE

durance   assurance   endurance   insurance

URBAN

Durban	turban	urban	suburban

URBER, URBAR

curber	Durbar	disturber	perturber
superber			

URBISH

furbish	Serbish	superbish

URCHASED, URCHEST

purchased
>   (*And extend* EARCH, ERCH, IRCH, URCH, *for* "birch-
>   est," *etc.*)

URDEN

burden	guerdon	Purdon	disburden
overburden			

URDER (*see* IRDAR, IRDER)

URDY, IRDIE

birdie	curdy	Ferdie	sturdy
wordy	hurdy-gurdy		

UREAU

bureau	Douro	Truro	futuro

URFY

Murphy	scurfy	surfy	turfy

URGENT

purgent	surgent	turgent	urgent
convergent	detergent	divergent	emergent
insurgent	resurgent		

URGEON

bourgeon	Sir John	Spurgeon	sturgeon
surgeon	habergeon		

URIOUS

curious	furious	spurious	Asturias
incurious	injurious	luxurious	penurious
usurious			

URIST, UREST

jurist	poorest	purist	tourist
caricaturist	(*And extend* URE *for "purest," etc.*)		

URKY (*see* ERKY)   URLY (*see* EARLY)

URLEW

curlew	purlieu

URMOIL

sperm-oil	turmoil

URMUR (*see* IRMER)   URNER (*see* EARNER)

URNET

burnet	gurnet	ternate	alternate

URNISH

burnish   furnish   sternish

UROR

furor   juror

(*And extend* OOR *and* URE *for* "poorer," "surer," *etc.*)

URRET

turret   "worrit"

URRIER

currier   furrier   hurrier   skurrier
spurrier   worrier

URROW

burrow   furrow   (*Compare* OROUGH.)

URRY

curry   flurry   furry   hurry
Murray   skurry   Surrey   urry
worry

URSAR, URSER (*see* ERCER)

URTAIN (*see* ERTAIN)

URTLE (*see* IRTLE), URVEY

purvey   survey

URY, EWRY, OORY

brewery   Drury   ewry   fury
Newry   houri   Jewry   jury
moory   Missouri

240

USCLE, USSEL, USTLE

bustle	Brussels (*for plurals*)		hustle
muscle	mussel	Russell	rustle
tussle	corpuscle		

USHER, USSIA

Prussia	Russia	usher	(*And extend* USH.)

USHY (*as in* "brushy")

brushy	cushy	gushy	lushy
mushy	plushy	rushy	

USHY (*as in* "bushy")

Bushey	bushy	wushy	pushy

USION

fusion	allusion	collusion	conclusion
confusion	contusion	delusion	diffusion
effusion	elusion	exclusion	extrusion
illusion	inclusion	infusion	intrusion
obtrusion	obtusion	pertusion	profusion
protusion	suffusion	transfusion	circumfusion

USKY

busky	dusky	husky	musky
tusky			

USSET

gusset	russet

USSIAN

Prussian	Russian	concussion	discussion
percussion	repercussion		

USSY

fussy   Gussie   hussy   pussy
"lawk-a-mussy"

USTARD

bustard   custard   mustard
  (*And extend* USTER *for* "*blustered,*" *etc.*)

USTER

luster   muster
  (*And extend* UST *for* "*duster,*" "*robuster,*" *etc.*)

USTFUL

lustful   trustful   disgustful   distrustful
mistrustful

USTIAN

fustian   combustion

USTIC

fustic   rustic

USTINGS

hustings   (*And extend* UST *for* "*dustings,*" *etc.*)

USTLE (*see* USCLE)

USTOM

custom   frustum   accustom

USTY

fusty   lusty   musty
  (*And extend* UST *for* "*dusty,*" *etc.*)

USY (*see* IZZY)   UTAL (*see* OOTLE)

UTHFUL

ruthful   toothful   truthful   youthful
untruthful

UTILE

futile   utile   inutile

UTION

ablution   absolution   allocution   attribution
circumlocution   circumvolution   collocution   consecution
constitution   contribution   convolution   dilution
destitution   devolution   diminution   dissolution
distribution   elocution   evolution   execution
institution   interlocution   involution   irresolution
Lilliputian   persecution   pollution   prosecution
prostitution   resolution   restitution   retribution
revolution   solution   substitution   volution

UTLER

butler   cutler   scuttler   subtler
sutler

UTNEY

chutney   Putney   gluttony   muttony

UTON

Luton   Newton   Teuton

UTTER

butter   clutter   cutter   flutter
gutter   mutter   putter   shutter
splutter   sputter   stutter   strutter
utter   Calcutta   rebutter

UTTLE

buttle   cuttle   scuttle   shuttle
subtle

UTTOCK

buttock   futtock   puttock

243

UTTON

button	Dutton	glutton	mutton
Sutton	unbutton		

UTTY

putty	puttee	tutty

(*And extend* UT *for "cutty," etc.*)

UTY (*see* OOTY)

UVIAL

pluvial	alluvial

UXION (*see* UCTION)   UYER (*see* IAR)

UZZLE

guzzle	muzzle	nuzzle	puzzle

UZZY

buzzy	fuzzy	hussy	muzzy
Fuzzy-Wuzzy			

YCLE

cycle	Michael	Lake Baikal

YLON

nylon	pylon

YMEN

hymen	flymen (*stage*)	piemen	Simon

YNTAX

syntax	tin-tacks

YPTIC

cryptic	styptic	elliptic

YPIST

typist	(*And extend* IPE *for "ripest," etc.*)

YTHAM

lytham	rhythm	Witham